With my Best

LATIF YAHL

2007

The
Black Hole

Latif Yahia author of "**I was Saddam's Son**" and "**the Devil's Double**" which have sold over one million copies worldwide in twenty languages now brings you the next chapter in his extraordinary and chilling life story.

ARCANUM

THE BLACK HOLE

Published by Arcanum Publishing in 2006.

1 3 5 7 10 8 6 4 2

Copyright © Arcanum Publishing 2006

First published in Ireland in© 2006 by Arcanum Publishing.

**Arcanum Publishing,
P.O Box 147,
O'Connor Square,
Tullamore, Co. Offaly,
Ireland.
www.arcanum-publishing.com**

Printed and bound in Ireland by Jetprint, Tullamore, Co. Offaly

Cover design by Michael Fedun and Alexander Six.
www.corrino.com

Photographs by kind courtesy of Latif Yahia and CBS, Karl Wendl, News

IRAQI MAP

ISBN 0-9554191-0-7

9 780955 419102

THE BLACK HOLE

I would like to give special thanks to my wife Karen and children without whose support and love this book would not have been possible. All profits from the sale of this book will be donated to the Children's Hospital in Ireland where my children were born.

Latif Yahia

- Introduction -

I would not be so presumptuous as to assume that every reader of this book has read The Devil's Double or Ich war Saddams Sohn [I was Saddam's Son]. It is possible that many readers will have approached this book hoping to learn more about the political and social aspects raised, particularly with regard to asylum seeking in general, or how the Saudi Arabian and Austrian administrations deal with dissent of any kind. For readers who have not read the story of how I ended up in Austria, or those who have read it and require a reminder, the following few paragraphs cover the same ground very briefly.

*   *   *   *   *

The geographically diverse land between Turkey to the north, Saudi Arabia to the south, Iran to the east and Syria to the west is rightly termed the cradle of civilisation. Ancient peoples such as Sumerians, Hittites, Babylonians, Persians and Assyrians cultivated the ground and were responsible for many of the technologies we now take for granted – the wheel being just one.

The wheel, however, came back to dominate the region; a worldwide wanderlust fed a human desire for transportation, which in turn needed fossil fuel to turn to smoke and make the wheels go round. And the area, now known as the Middle East, sits on trillions of tankfuls of the stuff. This underground resource has been the cause of much war, territorial dispute and conspiracy. After all, the hand that rocks the oil pumps controls the world.

Between 1979 and 2003, that hand was Saddam Hussein's. He would also use it to sign death warrants on dissenters, to murder his own countrymen, to plot disastrous wars with neighbouring countries and to be the puppet master of his entire population. In September 1987, Saddam – or more accurately, his son, Uday – picked up my strings. Uday wanted a double, and I was unlucky enough to resemble him.

This was not my first encounter with Uday. Because of my father's wealth I was sent to the best school in Iraq, and a young, spoilt, arrogant, Uday became our classmate. We hated him even then. He would cruise the streets in his cars and with the assistance of his bodyguards would pick up girls whether they wanted to or not – and most did not. At least one girl who refused to be taken by him was kidnapped and thrown to his starving dogs. In class he would act like his father, showing no enthusiasm for lessons and acting threateningly towards anyone who crossed him. A teacher who reprimanded him for bringing his girlfriend into class with him was never seen again.

My classmates used to tease me and call me Uday because even at that age I resembled him. I used to imitate him for laughs.

When my second encounter with Uday came about, I was a Captain on the front in Iraq's pointless war with Iran. My unit's command received a dispatch saying that I should be sent to the presidential palace. I was taken there and informed that I was to become Uday Hussein's fiday, or body double. This would involve attending functions, making appearances, and assuming his persona when rumours of assassination were circulating. Saddam had several fidays already, and Uday obviously longed for one just like his daddy, and I was to be his first. My initial refusal was met with a long spell of solitary confinement and mental torture in a cramped cell without so much as a toilet to maintain my dignity. Eventually, this treatment, and vile threats against my family, forced me to agree to Uday's demands.

Throughout a lengthy period I was trained to act like him and to speak like him; I was, through cosmetic surgery, also made to look even more like him. Indeed, having my front teeth filed down and being given a copy of his overbite-dominated set gave me a lisp just like his. I was, during my "training", desensitised to the ugly barbarity of the regime by being forced to watch endless, excruciating videos of real torture, mutilation and murder perpetrated by them on dozens of men, women and children of Iraq, usually prisoners or prisoners' family members. These films also served as a warning as to what I could expect were I to decide to challenge the regime at any time in the future.

My first public appearance as Uday was at a football match in Baghdad's People's Stadium. My job was to wave at the crowd from a dignitaries' box and present medals to the players at the end. When Uday saw the appearance on television he was impressed, congratulated my trainers and accepted me as a member of his circle, albeit on the outer reaches. He could not allow anyone to become too close to him, particularly anyone from outside the Tikriti clan from which the majority of the regime was drawn; indeed, I had been the first fiday to be plucked from the outside world. From then on my days were spent living in his palaces, effectively a prisoner, as I was not allowed to do anything without permission. But it was a prison of opulence and luxury, with access to the finest food and drink the world had to offer; swimming pools and other such charmed diversions made the time a little more bearable.

But the captivity grew stultifying. Most of the time I would not be making appearances; I would be bored out of my mind, intellectually and socially unchallenged. I had graduated with a degree in law and had dreamt of following in my father's footsteps and becoming a businessman. This had never been part of my master plan. I was largely living a brainless, useless existence with no independence or exercise of free will. Worse was to come. I got sucked closer to Uday and he started to treat me as one of his bodyguards, taking me out with him as protection against assassination at the hands of any of his multitude of enemies. This is when I witnessed the depravity of Uday at first hand. I saw him rape, murder, bully and destroy anyone who dared to question his will. This could be anyone from friends of his father to innocent passers-by, on one occasion a honeymooning couple, the wife of which Uday took a liking to and who threw herself to her death from her balcony after being raped by Uday.

3

Then came Saddam's invasion of Kuwait in 1990. This was a time when every warring tyrant needs a double, and I was put to good effect, visiting the troops in Basra posing as Uday, to show courage, fortitude and supposedly to improve morale, while all the time Uday himself was drunk in the safety of Switzerland. I was also pressed into plundering Kuwait, leading parties of thieves into car showrooms to steal luxury cars and take them back to Baghdad to be sold at huge auctions. But Uday was growing tired of me. When he was accused of plundering Kuwait and faced huge embarrassment for such actions he had the perfect excuse – that it was I who had stolen everything – and that he was completely innocent. I was made to "confess" on television – a ridiculous charade in a country with no electricity – and sentenced to death. It was of course a convenient cover. Uday had begun to sense that I was resisting his will, that I wanted to escape his clutches. I was saved by the beginning of the invasion of the US-led forces, which seemed to give the regime other things to think about.

Saddam was kicked out of Kuwait but survived politically, and my death sentence seemed to have been forgotten about. After a trumped-up row over a girl I was sent to a "re-education camp" where I was tortured and humiliated for weeks. That particular horror ended when Uday came to visit me one day, but it was replaced with another kind of horror. He had me shaved from head to toe and dumped on the doorstep of my parents' home. My mother discovered me but did not recognise the bald, skeletal figure at her feet until I spoke to tell her who I was.

I was later offered a sort of freedom, by way of gratitude for the way I had performed when called upon. But once again, at a party, I caught Uday on a bad day and he had me captured and held by his bodyguards while he went to sort out some business or other. I was sure that I was to be executed when he came back. I tricked my guard and made my escape to the north of Iraq, where I was captured and robbed by Kurds. But at least for the time being I was free from Uday. I eventually managed to flee to Austria, which is where my story picks up in this book.

Saddam and Family

When I wrote and published *I Was Saddam's Son* in 1994 and *The Devil's Double* in 2003, I thought that my story was finished, at least as far as the public interest was concerned. It went on to be a success and I would like to take this opportunity to thank all those who cared enough, or were shocked enough, to buy it. On fleeing Iraq I was penniless, and it helped financially as well as emotionally; it was also a priceless cathartic experience. As expected I received no plaudits from Uday or Saddam Hussein, and a good deal of this book covers my ongoing fight with them, particularly with Uday.

Throughout this book details emerge of assassination attempts, murder, emotional breakdown and moments of lightness which I hope everyone can identify with, but which also serve to put space between the extraordinary, brutal existence which I was forced to endure and the loving, productive life I yearned for.

The overall purpose of the book, however, is to reveal to the world a tiny sample of the injustice, exploitation and horror that are daily enacted from the highest levels of some of the nations whose representatives have no doubt shaken the hand of, or might even be, your president, prime minister or monarch.

I would never have believed, as I was being flown in the aeroplane from Turkey to Austria, that I was not escaping hell, but merely being moved to another of its fiery chambers.

*   *   *   *   *

The decision to write and publish this story was not an easy one to make. I cannot believe that the normal legal protection given to journalists, historians and biographers applies to me. I have been subjected to enough torture, kidnappings, imprisonment and assassination attempts whilst living in the jurisdictions of the free world to have any faith in the observance of international law. Some of the revelations herein will definitely not endear me to international, ubiquitous agencies who thought that they had shut me up long ago.

I spent many hours discussing the pros and cons of publication with my friends and family. I now have a young family of my own, and the responsibility I owe to them has never left my mind. Most of my friends advised me, as I thought they would, to let my story lie, let it fade away and carry on with a life which had become rather comfortable for me. They were, I believe, advising me from the heart, or from the gut feelings about the dangers to which I would be exposing myself and my family. They have continually reminded me that, despite the fact that I have lived in the European Union for the best part of fourteen years, I am still stateless, still effectively a refugee, and that no country had a duty to protect me or investigate my disappearance. I believe the stories I have heard about Iraqis voicing anti-war sentiments or criticising the US administration and being swept away in appropriately-named Gulfstream jets, never to be seen again, or re-emerging with more approved views.

Or perhaps the consequences would be less bad – I could be subjected to character assassination, ridicule and veiled threats. No doubt I would be branded a Walter Mitty, a fantasist, a conspiracy theorist, someone with an axe to grind or burdened with the weight of other uncomplimentary clichés. Government-sponsored journalists and reviewers would probably say I was pro-Saddam, a terrorist and a social misfit, and some of these assertions would stick.

Throughout the world, in the US, in Europe, in the Middle East and in the seats of power at the heart of "liberated" Iraq are people who could pull enough strings to have me written off physically, critically or credibly. My friends' arguments were convincing and sensible, and I decided to take their advice and keep my story to myself, at least until the dust had settled, some-time in the 2070s.

But then they came back. The **CIA** started to pay me attention and for some reason began to harass me interminably. Had someone been serving them false information about me, asking for certain favours? I can think of several potential originators of such actions, and the contents of these pages will provide readers with some of the many reasons why certain people would prefer it if this book did not make it onto the shelves, or if I were to be discontinued.

In my years since fleeing Iraq, I have plunged to suicidal low points and enjoyed the exhilarating highs that a good life can serve up. I have been in more embassies and governmental departments than I care to remember and have met world leaders and notables from all disciplines. If there is one thing that I have learnt, it is that the world's leaders act like a single family, rarely criticising each other unless a scapegoat nation is needed. They will turn a blind eye to each others' misdeeds, treating them as internal matters that are immune to international condemnation. What is more, they indulge in favour-giving deals in which millions of dollars of credit change hands. I have participated in it myself, and I have seen prime ministers and presidents shaking hands on deals that will never make the news. It would only take one of them to request that I should be silenced and it would be done. On the other hand, I have been impressed with the robustness of a few nations, most notably Germany, for whom the rule of law is not a structure to be toyed with, but is the immutable basis of all political actions, and a country where the legislature is as strong as the executive. It is often left out in the cold as a result.

Saddam and Rumsfeld in Baghdad 1983

So here I am, an anti-Saddam Iraqi escapee who has the audacity not to support Bush and Rumsfeld's Middle Eastern oil grabbing adventures. Along with billions worldwide, I disagree with terrorism and with military action on defenceless populations. I am not with the Americans and I am not with the terrorists, which leaves me as something of an outcast in George W's polarised, inward-looking world view. I remain opposed to Bush and his coterie of belligerents while not being opposed to America or Americans in general. This sentiment is again widespread, but for the most sinister of reasons I shudder when I express it, for I feel vulnerable. People fleeing Saddam's Iraq are not meant to oppose the present occupying forces in the White House and on Capitol Hill. After all, they were the guys who went and kicked his ass (or at least they sent the guys who went and kicked his ass). I am supposed to be eternally grateful. Because I am not, I must be a threat. I must be plotting against them. That is the polarised logic I am up against.

So in the end, my motivation for publishing this book came down to this fact: there is a truth that needs to be told, and if I do not tell it now, it might remain hidden forever.

Uday with King Abdullah of Jordan

Latif Yahia with the CIA in North Iraq 1991

- Preface -

In my book, *The Devil's Double*, there was no mention of the fact that I had with me a woman when I fled to Austria. However, as will become obvious, I had with me a woman named Nusa who was reported in the press and on television reports to be my wife. She was not my wife; she was one of the women who hung on to Uday Saddam Hussein and his inescapable opulent lifestyle – a hired girl, a prostitute. She had been introduced to me by Issam Malla, who was famous among the upper classes of Baghdad, a man who sorted out girls for the well-heeled members of Iraqi society. In the West he would be considered a pimp, but like most of the criminals who ran the country for over twenty years he was careful to maintain a public image of refinement and respectability. This image was maintained by his choice of clientele. Government ministers, businessmen and politicians linked to the inner circle were all enthralled by the radiance and beauty of his charges, their accessibility (at a cost), and the ego boost afforded by their company. He probably saw his business as a legitimate arm of the Western-influenced state that was Saddam's Iraq. And of course, he was right.

Issam used to visit me every Thursday – the equivalent of a Western Saturday or Sunday. He would arrange girls with whom my friends and I would socialise and be entertained. He would be accompanied by some of the girls so that we might choose a suitable partner for whatever occasion was taking place, or simply to spend time with. On one such occasion, he brought with him a captivating Shia girl named Nusa. I chose her to accompany me that night; she was good company. Over the following days she continued to visit me and we slipped into a tentative closeness that had never taken hold with previous girls provided all too easily by Issam.

In addition, Nusa and I had not known each other long; we were little more than acquainted when we effected our the flight from the cauldron of fear and hatred that was boiling all around us.

The decision to "rescue" her was mine, although her pleading was instrumental in my decision. I did not want to have anyone in tow. I trusted no one, and bringing her with me would increase my chances of capture. However, before me was a human being, one who had been sucked into Saddam's world just as I had been and whose very survival probably rested on my whim. I do not consider myself a hero by this action. It was a bout of humanity and normality that I had long been craving in my brutal, make-believe existence. The two of us went on to share experiences that will be related in this book, but ours was a fake "marriage" of convenience, which in many ways proved beneficial to both of us. However, the time is right for the truth to be told regarding her, and this book presents the ideal opportunity.

Apart from this detail, for which I hope the reader will forgive me, this story follows seamlessly from that told in *The Devil's Double*. Revealing her presence and her identity would have imperilled both her and the family she left behind in Iraq. There was no attempt to fictionalise or gloss over the truth for reasons other than this.

Latif Yahia with Nusa

I must also point out that several of the people who play their parts in this story have either had their name changed or have not been named, largely because they or their relatives are vulnerable or do not have the wherewithal to protect themselves from intelligence services and various other agencies from around the globe. They are the people who have had a place in this story thrust upon them by circumstance, rather than people who have sought privilege or position by entering the public domain. Some have confided in me and I will not betray their trust.

Conversely, there are names herein of people who have forced themselves into my life in the hope of damaging me physically, emotionally or professionally. Many of these have not benefited from anonymity. I am assured in the veracity of my story, and fear no legal action from such quarters under any law that I know of. However, one or two of those people who have caused me pain and suffering have been let off the hook somewhat because naming them would reveal the identity of someone whose anonymity I have sought to protect.

Uday and his father Saddam

- Chapter 1 -
A European Welcome

By the time of our flight from Iraq, early in 1992, Saddam's troops had been driven from Kuwait, the unconditional surrender had long been signed at Safwan Airfield by Lieutenant-General Sultan Hashim Ahmad and General Schwarzkopf, and the United Nations' "no-fly zones" were being enforced, but Saddam remained firmly in power.

The no-fly zones had the effect of severely restricting the Iraqi regime's ability to continue attacking the populations in the north and the south of Iraq (chiefly the Kurds and the Marsh Arabs, respectively). Both had suffered numbing oppression and terrifying violence at the hands of Saddam, his ministers and his armies. Kurdistan responded to the no-fly zone by becoming a quasi-autonomous administrative region, as Baghdad's ideological grip was ineffective without the free run of its military. However, it was, and still is, part of Iraq in the often arbitrary political geography of the Middle East. Its people's desire for independence is strongly opposed by Turkey, and Iraq is anxious to keep the Kurdish region as its own thanks to the large reserves of oil in the region of Kirkuk , the northern city which would be the capital of a state of Kurdistan were it ever to gain independence; after Saddam was finally overthrown and a new Iraqi government installed, Kirkuk became the capital of the Iraqi province known as Kurdistan.

To Nusa, the prostitute who had begged me to take her with me, and me, the north of Iraq represented a sort of freedom, a base camp for our flight from the country. After a frenzied drive from Baghdad, during which my rear-view mirror received more attention than did the view from my windscreen, we made it to the coalition-controlled Kurdish area and prepared to carry out our plans. I had posed as Uday on several occasions to ensure passage through checkpoints, a risky but vital strategy; fortunately, most of the checkpoint guards had been too terrified of Uday to pay me much attention.

On arrival in the Kurdish region, things stopped going to plan. We were robbed, taken hostage and imprisoned by the Kurdish Socialist Party, and several uncertain weeks were spent in cells and being driven and held at gunpoint before we finally made it to a US agent, who immediately set about arranging our escape. Ironically, the leader of the Kurdish Socialist party Mr Mammend and his second man Mr. Othman (who now holds a British passport) who personally oversaw and directed my torture in that dingy cell and later went on to shoot two men in front of me, Kurdish prisoners that Othman believed were working for the Saddam Regime one that held a German passport whose name was Kaled. (This proved later to be incorrect, but hey, they were dead anyway) Othman went on to become a major figure in the Post Saddam elected government after the invasion by America in 2003. A tribute to the fact that blood will never be too far away from Iraqs' door.

You can change the faces but the practices remain the same, wether they be Kurdish, Arab or Shi'ite. We were finally picked up by an American helicopter which took us further north to the relative safety of Turkey, where we made contact with other representatives of the American intelligence services, who were to arrange our next step.

Even at this point I understood that my return to Baghdad, and probably Iraq, would be impossible at least until the regime had been toppled, and was less than certain even then, such would have been the mistrust and detestation of anyone seen as being connected with Saddam and his atrocious sons. There was also the fear that my escape would provoke Uday, or, more accurately, Iraqi intelligence to be on my tail and that capture, torture and probable death would ensue. I was acutely aware of the danger in which my actions had put my family and acquaintances. It was something I would have to deal with, but such thoughts chilled me to a halt whenever they crossed my mind. Perhaps the degree of freedom I would enjoy would allow me to arrange something. Besides, I was far from safe even then. I did not know what lay ahead of me in Europe, how I would be treated or accepted, and for how long I would be there.

Furthermore, my status had, on crossing the Turkey–Iraq border, switched from an implanted member of Saddam's extended inner circle – with all the seedy benefits that that ensured – to that of a refugee, running for my life and relying on the openness and legal processes of the West. I was casting myself on a continent in the hope that its reputation for exercising compassion was true. (Time was later to suggest that the reputation is only partly deserved.) But rather than being afraid, I was filled with a sense of cautious optimism. A lifeboat might not be the best place to be in stormy seas, but it is preferable to being on a sinking ship.

I had been asked by the CIA about where I would be applying for asylum. Knowing little about Europe, I decided on Austria on the premise that I had a cousin there. He was a doctor and by all accounts was successful. As is the case all over the world, doctors are held in high regard by the people they serve. A respected contact in a foreign country could, I reasoned, soften my landing. Admittedly, however, my options were somewhat limited. Most of my friends and family were firmly rooted in the land I had fled.

There remained the fact that I would be of great value to America, the main protagonists in Operation Desert Storm and in the enforcement of the no-fly zones. Inside my head was an encyclopaedia of Iraq's dictatorship, its workings, its hierarchy, its palaces. In the United States I could have had an assurance of safety, which would of course be paid for with that knowledge. But I also knew that once my priceless resource had been exploited I would be on my own, probably looking over my shoulder, trusting no one – precisely the situation I was fleeing.

The inevitable offer of refuge came in the end from Dick Cheney, then the country's defence minister. But accepting his offer grated on me in a way which is difficult to explain. I had never had any cause to dislike Americans as individuals – I now have many American friends, and they have enhanced my life immeasurably. They have a stimulating enthusiasm and a straight-spoken honesty which I admire. The American people and their immigrant forebears have indeed imbued the nation with a unique sense of purpose, but it is a sense of purpose that does not always travel well, especially when it is driven home by force. They are like the person who can light up a social gathering but with whom one is glad one does not have to share a home. There is an otherness about America that attracts and repels in equal measure – the strength of instinctive repulsion roughly proportional to one's proximity to Babylon. Had I been able to choose between the American people and the American government, the choice would have been easy. However, I had to take both or neither; my decision was made.

To the American government's credit, their arm-twisting was carried out with a light grip, and they made arrangements with Vienna for me to be transported to Austrian soil to serve my asylum-seeking period. In order for the US to spring me from Iraq, I had to agree to certain conditions, one of which concerning what I knew about Saddam. I agreed reluctantly, as I had no idea how the information would be used. I was anxious not to harm the Iraqi people but cared little for what they had planned for Saddam and my ex-employer. The US could and would come and get me as soon as they needed the intelligence. It was not as though I would be fired into a black hole. Austria is a proud member of the brotherhood of nations, albeit one with a historical commitment to intercultural harmony as chequered as the Croatian flag. Hopefully that image had been consigned to history.

We were granted single-journey passports by the United Nations and on 9 March 1992, Nusa and I Arrived in Vienna. My immediate concern was that my cousin and I would not be able to recognise one another. We had not met since 1973, when I was a beardless nine-year-old with unmodified incisors and he was a young boy whose parents were embarking on an adventure in Europe, which in those days seemed esoteric, distant and modern to us. Perhaps the uncertainty of being recognised was the first sign that I had ceased to be Uday; the Latif in me was re-energising. Of course my cousin will recognise me, I reminded myself – he just needs to look for Uday in the crowd!

"Latif?" came the uncertain call from the collected meeters and greeters at the airport. "Latif!" he laughed as I spun my head in recognition. Latif – my name, but it sounded like the name of an old friend. We shook hands, kissed each other and hugged tightly. Here, in this city with its moderately northern climate and guttural tongue, was a warmly familiar link with my country. Sure, he had become used to Western ways, but the warmth of our greeting spanned continents in a way that only family or nation can do. By degrees, I was feeling safer, but this step seemed so meaningful that it was difficult to imagine myself in the clutches of the Saddamites again.

My cousin was introduced to Nusa and they greeted each other in a familial way. He was not to know that she was not my wife, although he no doubt made that assumption. Whereas in Europe having a mistress is frowned upon but accepted as what goes on, in Arabic countries it is a cause for great shame and even ostracism for both parties. He would no doubt have been aware of the cultural differences and, either through discretion or supposition, never so much as thought about raising the issue.

Leaving the airport, we got into his BMW and set off through Vienna. This city of beauty and drama slipped into our wake as we cruised through its streets. The architecture and general atmosphere were unlike those of any Iraqi city I had visited. The only word I could use to describe the place was "European" – pretty much as I had imagined, but striking nonetheless. The journey seemed to take quite some time, the buildings' grandiosity diminishing as we progressed, which suggested a suburban or even pastoral destination. This would figure, as successful city dwellers often crave the comparative peace and security of the outskirts when they tire of urban living. But the journey took us well outside the city limits, although I felt as though we were still in its orbit. We finally drew up in a town called Traiskirchen, situated about thirty kilometres south of the centre of Vienna. The town has an industrial feel to it but it is, I am told, well known for its viticulture; the eastern foothills of the Alps are visible to the south-east.

I noticed an enormous, looming building, and it soon turned out that the

"Traiskirchen" I would be staying at was not some suburban wine-growing idyll, but was the name of Austria's main refugee camp. My cousin had merely brought me to the place he had been instructed to. Where I come from, if you meet a relative after a long spell apart, it is traditional to be taken to his or her home, to take their hospitality for granted. It was a shock for Nusa and me to find ourselves here, and we were not overly reassured by the word refugee ¬– one finding refuge ¬– as the cold, dark, overbearing, forbidding appearance of the place brought less comforting thoughts to mind. There was also the point that neither Nusa nor I had any knowledge of German; under the assumption that we would be taken in by my cousin, this did not seem to matter compared to the urgency with which we were to leave Iraq. I could speak reasonably good English, however; maybe that would help. Many Europeans know a bit of English.

My cousin approached the security outside the building and started talking to the guards, returning a few minutes later with instructions to accompany him into the camp. It would appear that he was to be our translator. We gathered what belongings had not been stolen from us by the Kurds and stepped towards the gates which were a gathering point for uniformed men, probably police or immigration officials. Whoever they were, they stopped their conversations and eyed Nusa and me as though we were pieces of shit that had been trodden into the carpet. If they were intending to intimidate us, they succeeded. Considering the fact that we were supposedly entering a place of refuge, safety and security, this attitude did not augur well, but our fates were in the hands of this foreign force and we had no choice but to pass them without drawing too much attention to ourselves. Was this how all refugees were regarded in Austria? Time would tell.

The reception room was small, dirty and less than welcoming, and we spent almost an hour there doing nothing before someone came to take us in. After filling in forms and going about the business of registration and reception, we were ordered like dogs to go to another room, this time a much larger one where the essentials of refugee life – blankets, plates and such like – were literally thrown at us by the indifferent staff. "Take this, take this," they would chant as they did so. It was nothing more than a chore to them. All the eating utensils we caught were dirty, the bedding reeking of stale sweat and urine. This was the unwashed detritus of other poor souls escaping unthinkable acts in places less civilised than even here.

An anger began to simmer inside me. We were being treated as prisoners, criminals, parasites, scum, not people fleeing certain death and looking for a temporary sanctuary. Only the arrogant can act with such dispassion.

A policeman and my cousin accompanied Nusa and me on a fifteen-minute walk, at the end of which was another enormous building. As the doors opened we were confronted with the dismal sight of families and individuals, the elderly and children of many nations gathered in their little groups. There was a tumult of crying, shouting and talking, and the echoes of all three made it impossible to be heard and understood.

But the walk was not over. We were led to a side room, a smaller one, no larger than twenty square metres in area, where five families were accommodated with the absolute minimum of privacy or dignity. Each family unit had a double bed for the parents and a bunk bed for the youngsters. The policeman pointed at an empty bed and through my cousin let it be known that this was to be ours.

This I was not expecting. I do not know quite what I was expecting when I extracted myself from the crushing vice of Iraq, but sharing a tiny room with five families had not been a scenario that would have got much of a foothold in my imaginings. I was convinced that I had had assurance from the Americans with whom I had arranged my escape that I would be whisked away to a safe home where I could start afresh and live in safety. I did not feel safe here. I was assured by my cousin that this was not a prison, that this was a temporary holding place for newly arrived asylum seekers, that our case would be dealt with and that we would be found a more permanent place of residence. This was simply the way things were done in Austria, he concluded. His instructions, from an authority no lower than the ministry of justice, had been to the effect that he would pick us up from the airport and bring us here for administrative purposes.

Nusa and I put our things down on our bed and surveyed our surroundings.

I for one had grown accustomed to palaces and wide open spaces, and this was as far removed from that ideal as I could have expected ever to find myself. I did not expect a palace, but to stay in this room with little ventilation and indescribable smells that would make one's eyes water seemed inhumane, even torturous. The five other families were Iraqi Christians. One of the women was pregnant and each couple had two or three children. We were left with no choice but to endure the screaming and crying, to try to close one's ears and get some rest.

Before long I noticed that the adults among my room-mates were watching me attentively and seemed even to be cowering and holding each other protectively, their eyes widened with fear and confusion, their bodies twitching whenever I moved. My recent past suddenly lurched back into my consciousness. They thought I was Uday, that I had somehow tracked them down and that unspeakable horrors awaited them. The sensation lurched into me with burning intensity. It was all too much for me to take. I emptied my lungs with screaming and swearing, and punched the bed with a dismal loss of control. The situation, the dull, depressing reality of freedom from Iraq and all it embodied had got the better of me and my rage was unstoppable. No doubt this terrified those present even more, but what did I care? For the first time since boarding the helicopter in northern Iraq, I wanted to return to sailing through the monotonous unpredictability of the Baghdad compound. I started yelling to be taken back to the airport and placed back in Iraq. I wanted it like nothing else.

"Don't be ridiculous," implored my cousin, "you'll be killed."

I screamed back at him, "So be it, I'd rather die there, surrounded by my family and my countrymen than in this stinking shit hole of a place."

"You know that's not true, Latif," he said. My cousin was right; I could not go back. Longing for Iraq was like looking forward to a death sentence. But over the coming years I would long for that futile return innumerable times. "You're probably very tired and distressed. You need rest. Think about everything tomorrow. It's been a long day."

Perhaps it was his professional bedside manner, but my cousin calmed me down with the force of reason and reassurance. He said I would not be here long and that everything would be fine. He opened his wallet and drew out 300 schillings, and offered it to me so that we could make ends meet. Of the opulence with which I had been surrounded only weeks earlier, and of my untroubled, middle-class upbringing, I had nothing to show. This money and the clothes we wore were all Nusa and I had to our names. The wad of notes looked impressive and generous, but still I refused to accept it. I insisted on sorting myself out, just as I had always done. He stuffed the money into Nusa's bag, so it became hers, which solved that moral dilemma.

My cousin left, saying he would visit every to day to see how things were going. He left us in the room with the five nervous families.

With growing reassurance that I was not Uday, the mood in the room elevated to mere misery, and conversations were struck up with the Iraqi refugees. They told us about the quality of the food in the camp, that is, how it was a sickening, tasteless slop with the nutritional value and texture of mud. Nusa and I were soon to find out for ourselves, when the evening meal period initiated and we made our way to the canteen with our greasy, stained plates and cutlery. The gelatinous blob made a smacking sound as it landed on my plate, and I looked down at it with dismay. My palate had assumed a palatial refinement during my time chez Uday, but even those refugees from culinary environments less charmed than my own found the food a disgusting, sub-human gruel that would have had prison inspectors foaming at the mouth. But this was no prison. It was off the legal radar. Nusa and I did not eat for five days. Our stomachs became tight with pain.

One trait that is often ignored by countries who take in asylum seekers is that they are by their nature an enterprising, brave and opportunistic breed. They are, after all, the fittest who have survived, the ones who have, by means of guile, sacrifice or financial advantage escaped closed societies and brutal regimes to seek freedom or to spread stories of their country's ills to the enlightened world, in the usually vain hope that it will care. Instead of being welcomed and praised by the supposedly civilised, entrepreneurial states that take them in, they are often corralled, hidden away, scapegoated and subjected to abuse by their host populations, governments and media. History is written by the victors; that's a given. And the immortalised prisoners who fashioned gliders and other means of escape from whatever they could scavenge from World War II prisons will – rightfully – always occupy a proud place in the psyche of the victorious. But many of those arriving in the West by escaping from their often lawless home countries would not even have been able to confront those trying to prevent their escape with a fragile Geneva convention. As long as the world tolerates brutal regimes, families and individuals will always be risking all to escape them. So much as planning to escape from such a place could be a death sentence. If the comfortable ruling classes could only begin to imagine the plights of these beleaguered people, and appreciate the brilliant and treach-erous escape plans they have made, perhaps they would be treated a little more sympathetically – or even as heroes.

So here we were, among people from whom I would once have been perhaps a couple of miles in Iraq, but prevented by levels of security, walls and mistrust ever to meet until our flight paths crossed in this squalid prison masquerading as a kind of sanctuary. We were not allowed out of the doors until we had been placed in slightly less temporary accommodation I was not processed the next day. In fact, there was no sign of it ever happening. Many days and nights of drudgery were to follow, although after getting to know some of my fellow inmates a little, I felt a tiny bit safer.

My room-mates' trust was eventually earned, and one day they whispered to me that some enterprising inmates had breached the outside walls and turned it into a secret means of access and egress. This was a hopeful devel-opment. Strangely, it was not used so much as an escape hatch than as a larder or a works entrance; people did actually go out and come back with provisions, be they begged, borrowed, stolen or paid for. There was also work to be had in the bars and restaurants, and a thriving black economy had sprung up in the environs of the Traiskirchen asylum centre thanks to that hole in the wall. Inmates would often leave in the evening and return in the morning, unnoticed and unmissed. In a bizarre take on Michelin approval, we were even recommended a good, inexpensive restaurant. I became glad of the money given by my cousin, and my stomach moaned at me to get a move on.

So it was that one night we excitedly squeezed our bodies through the opening and marched, with our throbbing appetites driving us on, to the recommended restaurant. Our mouths started to salivate as we neared the place, the aroma of cooked food having been kept from our noses for so long. We ordered kebabs and sandwiches from the menu.

Communication was a problem. The filthy looks we had been greeted with by those guarding the gates to the camp proved not to be isolated sneers of paramilitary camaraderie, but a condensed, official expression of popular feeling. The people in Austria seemed to have an aversion to darker-skinned people that I have experienced nowhere else, least of all in neighbouring Germany. They made no effort to communicate. If I tried to speak in English they would reply in German, even when it was obvious that they had under-stood my questions. There were no attempts to reply with gestures or attempts to seek help from another passer-by. Perhaps it was the small-town attitude that comforts people all over the suburban world; maybe Vienna itself would be different. This first true experience of the Austrian general public gave me the impression that racism, mistrust and excessive defen-siveness were quite normal and acceptable attitudes in Austria.

As the palatable food digested, Nusa and I decided that the time was right to head back to the centre. I went to pay, but when I asked the price, the owner of the restaurant answered in an unintelligible German. I shook my head and asked for the price in English. He looked blankly back. I fanned out the 300 schillings under his face and told him just to take whatever the bill came to. I put the idea of leaving a tip on hold. My eyes widened as he took over 200 schillings. Exchange rates and such like had not really occurred to me; my cousin's donation had looked like enough to last a week, but it turned out that 300 schillings was roughly equivalent to twenty-five dollars!

The activities of the previous days had softened my cigarette cravings, but now that I felt a little more relaxed and had time to think, the desire for a few lungfuls of smoke reappeared. I asked the owner how much were the cigarettes; they were about 35 schillings. I bought two packets, thereby using up all the cash we had between us. Half an hour's living outside the centre's walls had left us penniless.

In view of the inmates' recommendation of the restaurant, I could only imagine that I had experienced the best of a bad brunch, so to speak. I would risk another establishment at my peril.

We found our way back to the centre and I made enquiries about what would happen next. I seemed to be going nowhere, despite what I had been assured. Our fellow inmates were surprised that we had not been told about the procedure. Full registration, we were told, was to be our next step in the asylum process; the form-filling on entry to Traiskirchen had been merely a preliminary formality. I already knew that, but had been expecting a call from an official to guide me through the next steps. But this was not the case, I was informed by a laughing room-mate. It was up to inmates to arrange their next step. Until then they were left, presumably as oblivious to procedure as I had been, in this appalling encampment. Full registration took place in an office in another building within the compound. The office opened at eleven in the morning but such was people's desperation to put the wheels of their cases' progress in motion that a queue started to form at 2 a.m. every day. It was intimated to me that without full registration I effectively did not exist.

That night Nusa and I got up at two and made our way to the office. It seemed that we were too late. The queue that had already formed was similar to that seen outside a football stadium on match day. It stretched all around the building. Estimates of how many people made it up would have been impossible, as the queue was thick in some places and thin in others, and its snaking nature made its length a matter of guesswork. Where did they all come from? I naively asked myself, before recalling that there were over twenty people in our compartment. I sighed as I took in the number of people in the queue I would have to join the end of. And this over eight hours before the offices opened. We made our way to the end, without much hope of being processed that day.

We slept as best we could. It was quite normal to sleep as there was no chance that the queue would move on for many hours; furthermore we had no possessions to be robbed of. The waiting was numbing, draining. Shuffling forwards commenced after eleven, and continued in tiny waves for several more hours. Because we would move forward a metre or so every five of ten minutes, it was impossible to get comfortable by sitting. Our backs and legs ached and our mouths were parched by the time we eventually made it to the door of the so-called interview room.

Here we had our second encounter with Austrian officialdom. A police officer of some unknowable rank sat on the chair with his feet on the desk, his shirt unbuttoned to the waist, contempt and boredom pressed into his features. He had the nonchalant bluster of the fictional dictator of every banana republic that has ever appeared in the movies. By his side he held an iron bar, more for intimidation than for emergency, one presumed. Here I learned my first useful fragment of my hosts' tongue: "Scheißeausländer" ("shit foreigner", I later found out). Unfortunately for him, I thought he was asking if I was okay or if I needed anything, or even welcoming me to his country. I replied courteously with a nod and a "Thank you." Could he have been testing my German language skills? I doubt it. I think he meant it. Whatever, he started to speak to me in a broken English. He asked where I was from, what was I doing in the country, the usual things. As the interview stumbled forwards, he became agitated at something and started banging his iron bar on the table as he bellowed questions at me and rolled his eyes when he could not understand my replies.. He was treating me with all the respect I would have expected from his greeting had I understood his language. A new anger was bubbling inside of me. This guy was nothing. He would not have lasted a minute if he ever adopted this attitude in Baghdad.

"Get me a translator," he yelled to one of his subordinates outside the room, smashing repeatedly on his tabletop with the bar. "What language are you speaking?"

I replied that I spoke Arabic.

He instructed one of his officers to go and fetch a translator and turned to me and said, "Now fuck off until we find an Arabic speaker.," He flicked his wrist at me, looked down at his pile of paperwork and seethed at it.

This belittling, dismissive comment and action ignited the rage inside me. I threw myself forward, got onto his desk and kicked him full in the face with the underside of my shoe. Blood immediately pumped out of his burst nose, and he fell back in agony. I could hear other policemen's heavy feet approaching, and at that moment noticed that the interviewer had been armed with a gun. I snatched it from its holster and grabbed the interviewer by the hair and pointed the gun at his head.

"If anyone comes a step closer," I screamed, "I will blow off his fucking head." The policemen's appreciation of English seemed to have made a gratifying leap and they stopped dead, looking at each other for a clue as to what to do next. I held him there, his ripped, bleeding head in my arm and his terrified eyes darting between me and the gun. I could sense the adrenaline coursing through me and no doubt it was a sensation he too was experiencing. It felt like I was Uday again, like I had an untouchable, unpunishable power. People simply did not speak to me in the way he had done, or treat me as he did. Perhaps Uday would have been proud of me.

The situation stagnated for about half an hour. My arm that held his head ached and shook. All actions in the centre had been halted while things were sorted out. Eventually a detachment of Cobra operatives arrived. Cobra is the special branch of the Austrian police who deal with terrorism and serious crime. They came wearing bullet-proof clothing and with a psychologist and his Arabic interpreter, ready to calm the situation. All very routine. I responded by placing a bullet in the gun, (no one had previously known it had not been loaded, which must have irked them), and yanking the interviewer's head back by his hair and thrusting the barrel into his mouth.

"I don't care what happens now," I growled. "If I pull the trigger he will die and so will I. Fuck you, fuck Austria, fuck the president and fuck everyone in this country."

There was intense chatter going on outside the room, and occasionally I thought I could sense a police siren in the distance, or maybe they were ambulances. Someone came in and took Nusa out of the room. I would not otherwise have had any recollection that she was still there, so focused was I on my hostage. The rescuers were asking her questions and I could hear her scared voice quivering as she responded.

After a minute or two of this, and careful instruction from whoever was directing operations, the translator came gingerly into the room and said, "It's okay. We know who you are. Who brought you here? You're in the wrong place. The Department of Justice had a place arranged for you. Let the man go. We will take you to the right place."
I refused.

After another half an hour, the secretary of the minister of justice arrived. He made pretty much the same offer.

"I'm not interested in your offer, and I don't believe you," I replied. "I came here by United Nations passport, and I want to be taken back to Iraq."

"We know all that," said the secretary. "But it appears that your cousin brought you to the wrong place. Let's sort this out and we can take you to where you should be."

"Fuck you and fuck my cousin and fuck everyone else!" I spat. I guess I had everyone covered by now. "I don't want to stay here."

The secretary adopted a conciliatory tone. "Look, let him go and nobody will be pressing charges. You don't know the law here, so we'll pretend it never happened. Just let the guy go. He needs help."

Still I refused. I insisted on being taken to the designated place. With my hostage. With the gun in his mouth. I trusted no one here. And so it was that I left the Traiskirchen centre with my finger on the trigger of a gun that was poised to eliminate my own personal *Scheißausländer.* We slowly made our way to the waiting car, passing fellow refugees (some of whom were, I like to think, willing me on) and the special police with their machine guns primed and ready to cut me down if I decided to end this official's days with his own gun.

Nusa and the translator got into the car. Once again the secretary of the minister of justice suggested that I let my captive go. Admittedly he was in need of treatment. "I don't trust you," I said, instructing the secretary to get into the front seat; I put myself in the back, still holding the interviewer's head. "I'll let this man go but I will have the gun pointing at your head until we get there," I told him. "No problem, OK," said the secretary, showing an admirable sense of bravery, irresponsibility or duty. "Just let him go." I slowly moved the gun from the interviewer's mouth to the secretary's head, and let the former go. "I'm here with you," said the secretary. "Kill me if you want, but you must trust me – we're going to the safe place."

The engine started and, as the main attraction of a convoy of six or seven cars, we made our way to the safe place, which was, I was to find out, in Vienna 13, the leafy residence of ambassadors, politicians and business people. The place I was to be placed in was not a luxury mansion; it was a small dwelling with a living room and a bedroom that was used by "higher-ranking" asylum seekers – fleeing politicians, political refugees and the like. Seeing the open spaces and then Vienna appearing along the road helped me to calm down. A perverse small-talk was started between the secretary and me, the kind that goes on when one of you is pointing a loaded gun at the other. I cannot remember a word of it, but I did grow to respect the man – even like him – and, more important, to trust him.

On arrival we were shown around. The place was small but it had everything we needed. Moreover, we were informed that this was only temporary accommodation and that one of the nearby larger houses would be ours just as soon as the present occupants vacated, roughly three weeks in the future. I nodded, but did not have much faith in the assertions of temporariness. Anyway, this house was a million times better than where we had just come from.

I handed the gun to the secretary, and apologised. I would have assured him that my actions had been out of character but I am not sure he would have believed me.

"Don't worry," he replied. "We understand your position and your motivation. Had any of the other refugees done what you did they would have got ten years' imprisonment. But since you are a special case, and you were brought to this country with the help of our government, and you were, as I said, taken to the wrong place. No charges will be brought against you and there will be no investigation."

I nodded. "What I would like, though," I said, "is for that man to be sacked. He is abusive to refugees, he treats them like dirt." I know little of what happened to the interviewer, and care less.

The secretary gave me a piece of paper with phone numbers on it, and said that someone from the government would visit twice a week. Then he left us to settle in. After Traiskirchen this modest house was like a palace. We had our own room, a shower, a kitchen. We could truly relax, reflect and plan for the future. The food was very good – halal compliant – and our hosts treated us respectfully.

We lived between a Turkish political refugee and an Afghan dissident who later was to become part of the first post-Taliban government in his country. Soon after we arrived they started to visit us and treated us as friends. Contact with my cousin was limited as his job in the hospital and on his rounds kept him busy most of the time.

Almost immediately I set in motion plans to get myself a gun. I made subtle enquiries about the possibility to my neighbours, and, although I do not know if they were armed themselves, I was given a few suggestions as to where I could find one. I was not prepared to put all my trust in Austrian intelligence or the country's police to protect me. I knew that Iraq's agents were ever-present. I quickly managed to get myself armed and kept the gun safe in the house, but hoped I would never have to pull the trigger in anger. So began my time of relative freedom. I was shaken and cynical after all that had gone on. And Austria seemed to be a reasonable place to live, notwith-

standing its uncertain welcome. At least we were not in Baghdad.
But was that a pang of genuine homesickness I just felt?

Latif Yahia in Northern Iraq with Kurds in February 1992

Saddam and Kurdish Mullah Mustafa AL-Barzani, the father of Masoud AL-Barzani the President of Kurdistan in Northern Iraq

- Chapter 2 -
Domestic Bliss Disturbed

The illusion of calmness settled into my days, and Nusa had began to enjoy her new life as an adopted European. Looking over my shoulder had been something I had grown used to over the previous years, so the lingering suspicions and paranoia were at their background levels, which was something I could cope with. We would visit our temporary neighbours and on occasion they would pop round to our house for a cup of coffee and an energetic conversation. With a little imagination, we could make out that life was approaching a suburban idyll, a level of normality that most take for granted. Naturally, I was eager to make plans for the future, of settling down somewhere. I was itching to start a business if at all possible, and I even let myself imagine starting a family.

At some point during this time Nusa had confided in me that she had a daughter, called Tara. She was not conceived in a previous marriage – or even a relationship. Tara's father was one of her clients in Baghdad (but not Saddam himself, as has been reported in certain newspapers), probably someone from the elite who would not have thought twice about bumping off Nusa and his unborn child rather than suffering the indignity of fathering a child to a prostitute. Nusa had found it necessary to keep the whole thing quiet; Tara lived in Karbala with Nusa's father. Although Nusa visited her as regularly as possible, because of her Baghdad lifestyle, and because the sprawling city was where she could be guaranteed some sort of income, regular visits were impossible. Still, while in Austria Nusa was suffering feverish pinings for Tara to the point where her mind became occupied only by wondering if she would ever see her again. Eventually, after several nights of desperation, she came out and asked me if there was any way we could bring her daughter over to Austria. How could I ignore this plea for help? Stuck in this strange, cold country, lonely, afraid and without possessions to call our own, Nusa and I undeniably grew closer together. We needed each other, both for comfort and by way of a guarantee – we had both staked our security in our flight, and if either of us had had second thoughts and decided to go back to Iraq, the other would no doubt have harmful consequences to face. Since we were living together, we considered it wise to fabricate the myth that we were married and that we had known one another for a couple of years. Back in Baghdad, the shame that would have been brought on me and my family from any marriage to a prostitute would have been unbearable, but such societal mores were a foreign currency over here. Besides, no one knew that she had been a prostitute. As a survival method it seemed to make sense to claim to be a couple. The authorities in Europe might think twice before dispatching with either of us were they to believe that we had large extended families back home. Moreover, my picture of Nusa was the same as it had been when I agreed to bring her with me – she was a terrified human being, not the lowly whore of the moralists and the extravagant ego-boost of her clients. Although she would in time cause me more heartache and anger than I would ever have thought possible, I find no profit in fretting about my decision to help her out.

At half past nine one morning, about a fortnight into our stay at our home, there was a knock on the door. I was pleased to see that we were being visited by my cousin, ecstatic when I noticed that he wore a smile and had with him a television set for us. It was a portable type; he helped us with the little aerial and we managed to get a decent picture. We had not had a television since we arrived, so the luxury it added to our lives was comparatively regal. The set, with a screen no more than twelve inches across, was like a surround-sound wide-screen home cinema as far as we were concerned, barracked in our home in this foreign land. He also gave us more pocket money – another 300 schillings. I vowed that I would repay him, but he turned my offers down with an affable shake of the head. The television had a grand total of three channels, all of them in German, but all day we sat and gazed at the pictures and listened to this impenetrable language, occasionally picking out the odd word and phrase that had become internationally recognised – Clinton, deutschmarks, OK.

The morning after the television had been delivered, at half past eight, a terrific banging on the front door shook the walls of the house, making the windows rattle. I dragged myself to the door and on opening it was confronted by a six-foot tall blue-eyed fair-haired man and behind him, dressed in suits, were about fifteen other burly men. I could not but be reminded of the Iraqi intelligence services – those respectable, businesslike men who brought with them nothing but nightmares for anyone unfortunate enough to warrant a visit. The man at the front introduced himself as Kessler, head of the Middle Eastern wing of the Austrian intelligence services; he wanted to talk to me. I invited him in. He seemed straightforward enough, businesslike and courteous, albeit in an domineering way.

Accompanied by five officers, he strode into the apartment. As I followed him in, I noticed that there were other agents in the back garden and when I looked through the front window I could see that perhaps five of the original backup team had remained in position, deployed such that the whole vicinity was covered, and communicating into their little microphones. There were also anonymous BMWs hurriedly parked up half on pavements and at disorganised angles – again, just like in Iraq. When you are on a swoop, there is no time for straightening the car up.

We sat down in the lounge, which suddenly seemed very small, dark and cramped with all these muscular men filling it. I offered them coffee but Kessler refused on their behalf.

"We need to know everything about you," Kessler announced, via an interpreter. "Everything. Who you are, what you were doing in Iraq, why you came here, what your job was. Everything."

"Let me just get changed," I replied, trying to be as accommodating as possible. Suddenly becoming red-faced and impatient, he told me to just come with him dressed as I was. I was in neither the mood nor the position to argue. In a column of vehicles I was transported to a police station, and taken up to the third floor where the staff were going about their business dressed in civilian clothing, like secret services or detectives. A room had been prepared for us and we paraded into it and the door was ordered to be closed behind us.

The moment the door crashed shut, Kessler ordered me to strip. I protested – nakedness, embarrassing in Western countries, is much more shameful to Arabs – but Kessler ignored me and told me that one of the men present was a doctor and that he had a few medical tests to perform to check my health. In this place resistance would have been futile, so I stripped, trying to maintain my dignity as best I could. The last time I had been forcibly stripped was by Uday; on that occasion I had also been shaven and dumped naked at my family's door. A sense of foreboding descended on me, but it was also a sense of captivity, of being the plaything of these people in whom I had no trust, and a great deal of fear. A humiliating, penetrating medical examination ensued. There seemed to be little going on of any medically beneficial nature; the tests were for something else, but I do not know what. They were possibly to get a sample of fresh DNA, but probably simply to belittle me. I had not had a chance to shower that morning.

I was allowed to dress, and Kessler and his men then embarked on a series of personal questions, starting with my date of birth and continuing through every aspect of my life. I considered it prudent to maintain that Nusa was my wife; Tara was introduced to them for the first time, and she was from now on to be presented as being my own daughter, Tara Latif Yahia. A wedding date was made up that would give credence to our claims on Tara. I committed it to memory; Nusa would never forgive me if I forgot our anniversary.

The questioning went on for four or five long, dry and hungry hours. Apart from the examination at the start, the meeting was reasonably civilised, with no aggression or violence, although I knew that it would surface the moment I showed the slightest hint of defiance. They had already proved their power over me when they had me undress in front of them and allowed a stranger to prod and examine me. I went through the motions without antagonising them and when I sensed that the interview was coming to a close, asked a question of my own: Could Tara be granted asylum and extracted from Iraq? The reply I got did not surprise me: Yes – if I would tell them all I knew about Uday. I agreed to tell them anything, although the knowledge that they were prepared to prolong the imperilment of this little girl in order to get intelligence (and, no doubt, personal promotion) seethed inside me.

All present agreed that we had done enough for the day, and that we would resume in two days' time. I was driven home. At my door Kessler gave me an envelope; I opened it and inside was two thousand shillings. I refused the money, for some reason thinking it was from Kessler's pocket. He laughed and told me that the money was from the Department of Justice and it was for us to feed and clothe ourselves and buy sundry items such as cigarettes. I signed for it, and suddenly felt like a millionaire.

"Get changed," I announced to Nusa after the throb of Kessler's engine had faded to silence. "We're going out!"

For two weeks we had not ventured beyond the end of the street, but with the stuffed envelope came an irrepressible wanderlust. I scribbled our address on a piece of paper and put in my back pocket so that if we got lost we could hand it to a taxi driver. Off we went into Vienna's centre, taking in the sights and buying a few basic items – tee shirts, underwear and such like. It is a beautiful city, dominated by the enormous, ornate cathedral and dozens of grand public and private buildings built during the opulent days of Empire. A feeling of euphoria overcame us when we started to appreciate the modern lifestyle exhibited by the populace over here. There was wealth and poverty just as in Iraq, but opportunity did not, at least on first impressions, appear to be determined by connections to some governing clan. The prosperity and comfort also came from peace. We had known nothing but war, violence, executions and fear, the kind of conditions hardly conducive to inspiring in a country's people enterprise and optimism. My eyes were opened. Very few police were about, and those that we saw were responding to calls or going about their beats in a casual way, which contrasted visibly with the intimidating, swaggering, trigger-happy manner in which the law enforcers prowl the streets of Baghdad. There were no intelligence services monitoring people's movements. It was a completely different world.

As planned, two days later Kessler rolled up and knocked on our front door. He said that we had an appointment and took me away again. This time we went to a different place, somewhere outside Vienna. It was a grand, plush restaurant, and the whole room had been booked just for us. We sat down to a luxurious meal, with excellent food and delicious drinks. Conversation was pleasant and felt in no way like an interrogation. In fact, we spoke of my past only a small amount. At the end of the meal, Kessler reminded me of my promise to give information to the Americans, by way of reimbursement for their removing me from Iraq. He informed me that the next time we met we would be accompanied by a US agent. "I am a man of my word," I replied, and agreed to the meeting.

And that was it for the day's meeting. I was returned to my apartment, again accompanied by three or four other cars with blue lights flashing, each vehicle full of agents armed with machine guns.

Another two days passed. The knock on the door came, and I greeted Kessler, who was this time accompanied by a short, fair-haired man. He was introduced as being from the American embassy. I invited them in, but again they had made other arrangements and I was whisked away to a beautiful hotel in the centre of Vienna. It turned out to be even more luxurious than the restaurant we had dined at two days earlier. There were four of us – me, Kessler, the American and a translator who was under the employment of the Americans.

Over delicious, expertly prepared starters we discussed Saddam, Uday, the situation in Iraq, and a host of other issues. I held nothing back, telling him all I knew. I had nothing to hide from them. The information might even benefit me if it led to Uday's capture or assassination. I needed to keep some things back, however. And I occasionally hinted that I knew more than I actually did, just to keep them interested enough to spare me.

After much procrastination, he came to the question of weapons of mass destruction – Saddam's fabled arsenal of chemical, nuclear, biological and radiological weapons. What they thought I, a virtual prisoner of Uday's, would know about such things I have no idea. But he asked about them anyway. I suppose he had to. I told him I knew nothing of such things.

"Don't start lying to us," he snapped.

"Look, I was not an insider of the regime," I explained. "Perhaps I have a small amount of information, possibly useless information, but if I were to let any of it out I would be killed for sure. I don't even know if it is reliable." There were certain top secret things I had accidentally been privy to, and it would have been obvious where the story had come from had it got back to Iraqi intelligence. They might have come after me with renewed vigour.

"We will look after you," said the American, with borrowed sincerity. But after six weeks in the country I was becoming accustomed to their condition-al hospitality, and considered it likely that I would receive no protection once I had exhausted my most exchangeable currency: my knowledge.

Nevertheless, I decided to play his game. "What guarantees will I receive that I will be looked after?" I asked. "How do I know I won't give you information and be kicked out of the country and sent back to Iraq? I know how the West supports Saddam and how people have been kidnapped and returned to the regime with European governments' blessing."

He faced the table and cleared his throat with an uneasy cough. "So what do you want?" he enquired.

I had my reply ready. "I want my presence in this country, and details of my asylum application, to be put into the national newspapers. And I want assured asylum. Then I will start talking."

The American looked over at Kessler, then back at me. Kessler said, "And if we give you asylum – how will we know you will help?"

I told him he could trust me, and that I was no friend of Uday's. Right on cue – in fact, as though we had been observed by the kitchen – the main courses arrived. Just as had been the case during the previous meal, once the main meal arrived our official business was not discussed at all. We made small

talk about the weather, about sport, about travel. Again I was escorted back
home in a convoy and given two thousand schillings by Kessler. I took it
without question this time; I needed food, cigarettes and clothes. A week
later, Kessler arrived with an envelope, this time containing not money but
my asylum approval certificates. I was granted political, not humanitarian,
asylum. This was a rare thing in Austria. The people with whom I was
living at Traiskirchen would all have been humanitarian cases. The forms
were in German; I shrugged my shoulders and Kessler indicated to me that
the two back pages were in Arabic. I took in the words for a few moments.
Kessler then told me that we were going to be taken to the Department of
Justice where I would present my letter and receive full asylum, plus identification and travel documentation. Nusa and I were beside ourselves with
joy and relief at this development. We would now be able to make a real start
and, more important, particularly for Nusa, we would be free to attempt to
get Tara out of Iraq to Europe, where she would undoubtedly be safer and
have a brighter future .That day we were officially granted political asylum.
At the Department of Justice we received our documents, and registered
Tara as our daughter, with the name I had given at the first interview with
Kessler.

We then went to the passport office. Nusa was immediately given a passport, but there did not seem to be one waiting for me. When I asked why, I
was told that it was because the passports were allocated on an alphabetical
basis, and that since N came before Y in the alphabet, mine would necessarily come long after hers. I found this explanation very hard to believe, yet
there was little I could do about it. Nevertheless, as an officially recognised
asylum seeker I knew I had at least a degree of protection, however small.

At around this time the house we had been promised became available, and
we were moved there as soon as it had been cleared. It was much more of a
homely dwelling, and a step closer to the airy, spacious quarters I had
become accustomed to in Baghdad – not that I expected or wanted that
again.

Every few days, Kessler would visit. He would take Nusa and I out for a
meal and we would talk about anything but Saddam, Iraq, Uday or chemi-

cal weapons. Instead he would show concern as to how we were, what we were up to and whether everything was working properly. He was, in his transparent way, trying to gain our trust. I never got the impression that we would ever become friends, and conversation was often awkward and wooden.

One morning, my cousin arrived, accompanied by the secretary of the minister of justice for the Middle East, Mr Zadeh. My cousin told me that he was a close friend of his. They were both affiliated with the ministry, my cousin in the capacity as a spokesman for Jalal Talabani (a Kurdish separatist leader, later to become president of the post-Saddam Iraqi government). It was a part-time position for my cousin, which he filled when his medical duties allowed.

The purpose of their visit was not social. They had been sent to me to request that I did not appear in the media, did not tell anyone who I was and generally to keep a low profile. Their reasons were clear; as soon as a journalist got so much as a sniff of the fact that I, Uday's *fiday,* was in Austria, my face and my story would be on the front page of every newspaper. Were that to happen, there could be no guarantees on my safety, for one reason more than all others: the Iraqi secret service was remarkably active in Austria and the two governments had a special relationship. (At the time, with Saddam flouting his UN-imposed surrender conditions, very few countries had an Iraqi embassy. Austria and Switzerland were the only two European nations to maintain diplomatic links with Iraq. These were links which ran much deeper than the thread of communication required to be information conduits, however, and guaranteed commerce, security and intelligence matters could go on as normal, although neither country's government would openly admit it. It is these illicit, opportunistic relationships that have kept many a vile dictatorship propped up long beyond what was natural.) I was also told to avoid travelling to the city centre, as this was where the embassy was situated and agents and informers were rife and had a degree of immunity, thanks to a central Austrian government who would turn a blind eye to any transgressions. The problem is that the embassy in Vienna is located rather like Iraq is situated in the Middle East – it is almost impossible to avoid passing its sphere when travelling from place to place;

avoiding it would in fact mean avoiding the city itself. My guests also suggested that I should shave off my beard – looking like Uday would be something of a giveaway – and to try other ways of altering my appearance. While grateful for the intentions of such advice, I regarded the proposed measures as a sort of defeat. I was supposed to have escaped all that, and if I had to live out my days in fear and suspicion, I would have been better off staying in Baghdad. My face was my face after all, and I did not want to change it. What is more, I had by then visited central Vienna on several occasions without turning heads or feeling suspicious of anything. As far as the media were concerned, I had no plans to make any major appearances, although my desire to be mentioned in the press without fanfare still remained.

We became more settled, and apart from the outstanding matter of Tara, began to grow happier, and less regretful of leaving Iraq. The number of acquaintances we had slowly grew, and through my American and Austrian contacts I would occasionally communicate with notables as they dropped into the city. The Kuwaitis and Saudis, like most nations in the diplomatic sphere, liked to celebrate national days and such like with invitations to the business world's local expatriates or other Middle Easterners. It was a means of social networking and little more. I was invited to several such events, and at one I met the leading Austrian statesman Kurt Waldheim, who had been president of Austria and then Secretary General of the UN in the early 1970s. In what was a very brief encounter I asked him why the Iraqi embassy was allowed to flourish in his country when the rest of the world had chosen to reject such links and thereby limit Saddam's reach and air of respectability. "Business is business," he said to me, with a playful pat on the shoulder and moving on to patronise another guest.

These ambassadorial events became more regular as time went on. At each event, business cards would be given to every ambassador and minister, and the card would be one's guarantee of invitation to their own gatherings. I found the meetings rather tiresome; the same conversations would be had countless times, and everyone seemed to be probing for information or business contacts with which to further their own standings. But I continued to attend nevertheless, as I could also occasionally get snippets of information from people connected with Iraq, talk of which was always keenly listened to. Many of the things I heard I did not believe, but some of it was useful. No two diplomats really seemed to trust each other. Everything for them was a game, but one that had to be learnt.

During this period, and continuing well into my future, I was visiting a psychiatrist, Dr Wolfgang, who was attempting to counsel me and help me to come to terms with what everyone but I knew was a traumatic experience that would without treatment come back to haunt me. He was a good listener, as they say, and put me sufficiently at my ease truly to open up to him and talk like I previously did not know how about my time in Iraq. Indeed, back home the idea of visiting a psychiatrist is tainted by the belief that it is a last-resort attempt to avert the onset of madness, or to pacify the already condemned. Counselling as such was seen as a quaint and unnecessary measure, partly because in times of trouble the society one belongs to is meant to offer support, and partly because one is supposed to simply get on with life. Iraq is teeming with traumatised souls, the legacy of three major wars and a brutal, uncaring leadership. Maybe feelings will change in time, and some help might be extended to them. I cannot begin to say how much Dr Wolfgang's counselling helped me, and dread to think what kind of person I would be today were it not for his professionalism and expertise.

As I have mentioned, one of the first things I had done when I arrived in Austria was to get hold of a gun. It felt completely natural to me – in Iraq, almost everyone has a gun, and it is considered strange not to own one, even if it is left at home. Quite apart from the danger I knew I was in, I felt somehow incomplete without one. Ownership of a gun is a sign of manhood, of responsibility and of a readiness to protect one's society in most Arabic regions; in Iraq it was a virtual necessity, thanks to the lawlessness that was rife in certain areas. So it came as something of a culture shock to be told that gun ownership in Austria, indeed over much of Europe, was itself something of an oddity, restricted to enthusiasts, farmers, gangsters and psychopaths, and the continent had many individual laws to protect against proliferation. This is a good thing only if there is strong protection given to the populace by the police and by the law. An unarmed population can be much more easily manipulated by powerful regimes, although it can also create a violent culture of its own, a jungle mentality. A well-armed population never saved Iraq from oppression, of course.

I had some very rational reasons for wanting to keep hold of a firearm of some sort, reasons that would need some serious dislodging. I was still a hunted man and I simply could not know when I would need it. Dr Wolfgang, with enormous skill and patience, managed to talk me round to a state where both my Iraqi mindset and my personal anxieties were erased to the point where I felt I could safely disarm. It is difficult to express how large a step this was for me, but I knew I had to leave behind the brutality that was the norm in my homeland if I was to successfully take on a new life as a European.

At first, my psychiatric sessions took place once a week; I was nervous and mistrustful, and could not see how they could be of benefit. Dr Wolfgang was incredible. I started to accept his help more often, which would raise eyebrows were it not for the fact that after a couple of weeks he refused to take any payment from me. Our relationship changed from a professional one to a strong friendship which continues to this day.

*   *   *   *   *

Vienna is famed for its coffee houses where afternoons can be wasted sipping the stimulating drink and sampling the array of savoury and sugar-coated cakes and pastries served apparently everywhere. Such places are impossible to miss, and at times it seemed like there was a coffee house for every inhabitant. We reasoned that it would have been a shame to come all this way without sampling the city's fare – that would be like going to New York and not visiting a sushi bar. So with a small amount of cash in our possession, we headed one day into the city centre, as excited as children before a birthday, only in our case at the prospect of tasting pastry! We were struck by the cleanliness of the place The locals were rightfully proud of their striking city, and it was not uncommon to see a passer-by picking up a piece of litter – almost certainly dropped by an outsider or blown in from another town – and putting it in a bin. I continue to feel an affection for the beauty of Vienna, if not for its motherland's flawed and often prejudiced psyche.

We made our way into to a cosy looking coffee house and sat down to eat and drink. I started talking to Nusa in Arabic, and when the waitress heard us she leant over and said, in a muted, surprised voice, "You are Iraqi?" She must have recognised our accent. Her eyes were wide open and seemed welcoming, but there could have been a hint of surprise, or even fear, in them.

"I am," I replied.

"So am I!" she responded, with a friendly smile. Then her tone changed, almost to an apologetic one. "You know, when I first saw you from over there, I thought Uday Saddam Hussein had walked in."

My body tensed and I said nothing. I had not practised a way of volleying back such comments. I simply did not know how to react, and probably looked quite uncomfortable in my attempts to look unemotional and blasé. Of course, the waitress's observation was not as unbelievable as it might have sounded. Uday would spend time in Europe, on business or simply for entertainment, although it must be said that it is quite unlikely that he would walk around a city like Vienna without some form of personal protection.

The waitress quickly changed the subject, and started to ask about how long we had been in Vienna, where we were staying and how long we would be staying, and such things. I told her we had been there a few months, and we did not know what we were going to do next. I could not trust even her, so limited my answers to the minimum of information and peppered them with exaggerations, understatements and plain untruths.

Her name was Juliette. We exchanged addresses and over the coming weeks became friends, although I tried to keep her at arm's length. She seemed to ask rather a lot of questions that had little to do with the conversation we were having. Nevertheless, it was refreshing for Nusa to have some female company, but I too was glad just to have another person to communicate with.

(It was only later that I discovered that during our friendship with Juliette, the Austrian intelligence services had been monitoring Nusa and me very closely. I was at one point advised by an agent to break off our friendship with her, because they had information that she was working for Iraqi intelligence. I also found out another explanation for her closeness to Nusa: by day she worked in a café and by night she was a dancer and a prostitute. Whether they knew each other's background or whether there was an instinctive bond between them I do not know. She was a Christian and her dream was to go and live in America, but somehow she had got stuck in Vienna and was almost certainly forced by circumstance into her various underground activities.) Juliette took us to an Egyptian nightclub, the owner of which I also got to know quite well. It was reassuring to see that someone from that general area could overcome prejudice and steer a business towards being reasonably successful. Once again my Arabic-speaking circle of friends had expanded a little, and I was beginning to become more settled.

On one of her visits, Juliette brought with her another Egyptian friend, William, who was a photographer for an Austrian tabloid newspaper. Like me he was about thirty and we got on well. But Juliette seemed to have a specific reason for bringing us together. She said that she had an instinctive feeling that I had a story but that she did not know for sure what it was. There was something about me, she believed, but confessed that she could not put her finger on it. I must have given something away, I suppose. How else is it possible to tell that someone has a story? It is not easy to keep one's guard up constantly. Or perhaps it was simply the fact that we had been housed in this particular part of Vienna, rather than in the kinds of places reserved for typical refugees. She let me know that if I wanted to air my "story", William could help me. He had connections in the press, she said, and could act as a go-between in any dealings. It was an offer I was interested in, but I considered it a little early just yet. I declined, but took his contact details just in case.

Nusa's pain at being separated from her daughter was acutely affecting her at this time. She wanted to hold her more than ever, to see her growing up and to free her from the drudgery of Iraq and introduce her to a new life like the one she herself was growing used to in Europe. She would cry every night, and before long she started to blame me for bringing her out of the country. I considered this unfair – she had begged me to take her with me – but I had no difficulty understanding what she was going through. I was missing my family too, and remembered how much I had missed them when I was ensconced in Uday's palaces; but perhaps I lacked somebody to blame, and she had me to act as her emotional punch-bag. Nevertheless, her constantly placing responsibility for every ill at my door, and her attempts to pin on me her own sense of guilt, caused me to snap and on one occasion a blazing row ensued. We had the kind of tumultuous row that can only take place between two deeply frustrated people. We screamed and shouted at each other just to be heard, but my tone must have terrified her, because after a particularly heart-felt scolding of mine she went straight to the phone and called the police.

Within minutes a policeman and a policewoman were banging on the door, and I was arrested and taken away to spent the night in a cell, purportedly for Nusa's safety. I passed the long night on a hard bench-like bed, barely sleeping, just lying there becoming progressively more infuriated at Nusa's overreaction. I was released the next day without charge, but was unable to contain my fury with Nusa. When I got back home I exploded, shouting, *"We need to stop seeing each other today! You're just a whore. I don't want to see you again. I could kill you. I'd bury you in the garden and nobody would miss you …"* Even I did not know whether I meant it. I was shaking.

She phoned the police again.

This time I spent two nights in the cell. I received a stern warning: next time, I would go to prison. I realised I needed a break from Nusa. And, I dare say, she needed some time away from me. What we had in common – our similar recent pasts – was not sufficient to hold together a relationship, and had we been in Iraq I doubt if our friendship would have had much mileage even if she had not been a prostitute.

In a way, I could blame my simmering rage on the state of frustration and helplessness I was suffering from. A day never passed when dreams of home – my birthplace – did not stop me in my tracks and force me to choose between the impossible and the undesirable. My stay in this country was never meant to be anything but temporary, although I always knew I had to stay here through lack of other viable options. My dreams would carry me away; in them I would be floating down the Tigris, my friends waving and calling me to come ashore, where we would talk about nothing until the orange setting sun would illuminate their faces then we would go on talking some more, until it rose again. We would often talk like this, throughout the night. But I had to snap out of this fantasy a hundred times. I am the absconded double of one of the world's most ruthless and depraved men. Returning to Iraq would mean death. Probably not just for me, but for my family, too. My being here was keeping them alive – human shields, bargaining chips, call them what you will. Baghdad must remain a dream, at least for the time being.

Every week or so Kessler would turn up at my door and give me an envelope full of spending money. He had also given me a mobile phone, the number for which was to remain a secret known only to me and his agency. Under no circumstances was I to use it for social reasons, but in an emergency I could be contacted by – or make contact with – Kessler. It was rarely used.

One day, in June 1992, the phone did ring. I answered it and a man introduced himself with his name and said he was from the American embassy. Before he could make his point I hung up and got in touch with Kessler; he said he was expecting someone to call and that I should talk to them. About two hours later the embassy called again. The man said that he would send a car for me which would take me to the embassy where they wanted to talk to me. I could see no harm in doing so.

A few hours later I was in the embassy with the American ambassador to Austria and several representatives of the CIA. They were asking me the same old questions – chemical weapons … Saddam's hideouts … weak spots … personal security … *et cetera, et cetera.* I reasserted to them the fact that I knew nothing, that I was never part of the inner circle, that I was merely the bullet-catcher of a dictator's playboy son, and that I had told them all I knew. I do not think they believed a word I was saying.

Eventually they changed the subject. They reminded me of the agreement we had made as a condition of my being plucked from the north of Iraq – that I would assist them with anti-Saddam activities. They had an additional request, something I might be interested in but that would, I was told, be of great assistance to the people of Iraq.

It transpired that in a few days' time an important conference was to take place in Vienna. It was to be a meeting of all the Iraqi opposition groups – a gathering of regional, political and religious concerns – and they would use the conference to find their common ground, assess their levels of support, plot a means of overthrowing Saddam and to make arrangements for taking over the reins of power once he was gone. It was effectively an unelected government in exile, made up of often self-appointed figureheads who happened to have the right blend of military and financial back-up. None of them had any popular support in Iraq, which was no surprise considering the fact that any opposition manifesto would become a suicide note, but there was an arrogance and presumptuousness in the current crop's invented, self-imposed status. I was invited to attend the conference and to choose which party I would be allying myself with.

"I don't want to get involved," I told them. "I want nothing to do with politics."

It was not the response they had expected. With surprise on her face, the ambassador said to me, "You know all about Jalal Talabani, don't you?" I replied that I had only heard of him, that I had never met him. This was not strictly true. I had met him, although he might not be so sure that he had ever met me, Latif Yahia. In fact, when we did meet in 1990, he was under the impression that he was meeting Uday, and thought that the 25-million-dinar donation – then approximately 25 million pounds – was a fitting gift for whatever services he had rendered. I did not need to know the specifics – I was not Uday. This was a man who the West thought was strongly

47

opposed to Saddam, but who would gladly do favours for him and for the regime. Did the donation go straight back into anti-Saddam party funds? Somehow, I doubt it. He had a lifestyle to maintain.

"You met him in Baghdad," she said, rousing me from my reverie. My mind flashed back to the present. "And you're going to meet him again at the conference. We will send a car to pick you up every day of the conference and you will attend. Your presence will boost the general morale of the conference. You survived the regime." She then handed me an envelope. I did not have to open it to understand that it contained money.

"I'm already getting money from the Austrian government," I said, sliding he envelope back to her.

"We know; this is extra. This is a gift from the American government." She slid it back my way.

"I'm sorry," I insisted. "I don't want any money. I have money." There was no such thing as a gift in my life at the time. There were only purchases and bribes. And a gift from the Americans was to be suspected more than any other. I knew about things their satellites, spy planes and secret agents did not. But I had no plans to sell my knowledge. I did not want any more bombs and cruise missiles careering through the Baghdad skies. I would gladly give away information to people I could trust with it, but sell it? That was official opposition territory. I pushed the envelope back to the ambassador.

"Just open it," she said. I refused. "Well I'll open it for you," she sighed. She opened it up and counted the money in front of me. One hundred thousand schillings.

"So what?" I said, with studied nonchalance. I would have been able to put that much money to good use; our regular contributions hardly kept us in luxury. I just knew that they were trying to buy me, and it would have been the start of something I would not be able to get out of. Had I taken the money I would have been under their control until they had finished with me. Every one of the groups gathered at the conference would have been financially sustained by various interested countries. By way of recompense, I gave a tentative agreement to at least attend – although not necessarily to contribute to – the conference, even though I considered it nothing more than the coalition of the billing.

Two days later the car arrived as planned and I was driven to the conference, which was taking place in one of Vienna's luxurious hotels overlooking the Danube. My efforts to keep a low profile proved pointless – on entering the hall heads started to turn in my direction. Gathered there were all the big players in what the West thought were the anti-Saddam organisations, including Ahmed al-Chalabi, who was for a while America's great hope for post-Saddam rule, despite his criminal past (in a way echoing Saddam's own rise). Present also were representatives of various Islamic groups, of Kurdish parties and of a variety of smaller interests, each with one goal – to get rid of Saddam and to start ruling themselves. As the day progressed, I was courted by members of virtually every group present; they saw me as a potential asset, as someone with inside knowledge of the clan, someone who would lend extra weight to their campaigns, boost the donations made to them and give them a greater share of power once it was redistributed by whoever overthrew Saddam (i.e., America).

The gathered hopefuls each had a paper-thin claim to power. The factions had little in common with each other, which would not necessarily be a bad thing in a nationally representative, post-dictatorship government, but the one desire they shared – to overthrow the regime – was enough to get them all in the same hotel for a couple of days. Each party would receive funding, usually from a sole sponsor state, which they would use to publicise their cause and, where appropriate, to improve themselves militarily. The amount of funding, and the importance of the state which chose to support them, would usually rest upon the numbers of loyal supporters they would claim to have in Iraq. In truth, support for all the gathered parties was negligible, which was as much because of Saddam's grip as because the characters involved were pretty unremarkable and generally untrustworthy. So they would make up the figures. They would claim a thousand supporters here, a couple of hundred there, and impress potential sponsors with their fantasy power bases which would pay dividends once Saddam was overthrown and rebuilding contracts were being drafted. It was impossible to check up on their claims, as nobody in Iraq would admit to affiliation with any anti-Ba'athist faction. In the meantime, the donations that were meant to be propping up grass-roots support within Iraq simply vanished, no doubt hidden away in secret accounts, ready to be accessed once a liberated Iraq had been bled dry. We are not talking thousands of dollars here, more like hundreds of millions.

So where would I fit into this arrangement? I had a definite position. I was avowedly anti-Saddam, and had, to a degree, a certain publicity value because of my past and my extraordinary access to the regime's workings. In short, I could be worth a few million dollars extra to the party, just as signing a well-known striker will add a few pennies to a publicly-owned football club's value. I was also an information bank who could be used to make useful and timely withdrawals, not to benefit any cause, but to give sponsors the impression that the party's spies were active and productive, even though there were no spies. (One example of their ignorance was later to emerge concerning the presence of the second wife of Saddam Hussein. Not a single party even knew she existed until my first book was published, after which her name would crop up with regularity in party statements.)

Al-Chalabi himself kept in the distance, but eventually approached me. I suppose he had been expecting me to make the first move towards someone of his imagined stature. He had two girls with him, which made him look more like a departmental manager at an office Christmas party. At length he asked me to join his group and work for him and the Iraqi National Congress, a group apparently modelling itself on Nelson Mandela's African predecessor, in ignorance of the fact that the average person in Palestinian Street would know nothing of their existence, let alone proudly wear their colours and pray for the day when they would take power. They were another fantasy opposition party, but they existed only in their own minds and on the payrolls of their sponsors.

"Good day, Mr. Yahia," he said, holding out his hand. "At last we have a chance to talk."

I took a long look at al-Chalabi and said aloofly, "Sorry, I don't know you."
"You must have heard of me," he said, glancing awkwardly at the girls at his
sides. "I am Ahmed al-Chalabi!"

"Yes," I shrugged, "Okay. I've heard of you. I've never met you, though."

"It's good that we have met, don't you think? We could do with someone
like you fighting for us."
He must have sensed my reluctance to get involved, and it unsettled him. He
was the centre of this particular universe and everyone knew they had to get
close to him if they were to consider themselves entitled to a slice of the Iraqi
pie. Were things to go his way he would be my president in several years'
time, so it must have irked him to see my indifference to his advances.

"So?" he at last ventured. "What do you say?"

"I say no," I replied, with a shake of the head and a bored glance around the
room.

(I was later to find out that the pimp who sorted out his girls got himself a
place in the post-Saddam interim government, a fact that served to demonstrate just how far Iraq had progressed after the dictator's fall.)

Next to shake my hand was Jalal Talabani of the Kurdish Democratic Party.
At least this one had done his homework. "Latif, you have Kurdish blood,"
he informed me. "We knew your grandfather, and he was a good man. Our
cause is the one you must naturally follow."

I told him I would think about it. I would also think about what my lineage
had to do with my political views. My cousin, the doctor, was present at the
conference in his position as Talabani's spokesman, so maybe there was
something in my genes that told me to follow this guy. Then again, there
was something in my genes that made me look like Uday, so perhaps my
genes and I could agree to differ on one or two issues.

Latif Yahia with Jalal Talabani 1991
(President of Iraq in Post Saddam government)

I attended every day of the conference, during which my bullshit detectors almost became habituated to the background stimulus. The third day was set aside for deciding on an interim opposition parliament in exile – a prime minister, a president, governmental posts and such like – which would assume control after Saddam's fall and thereby maintain law and order and set in motion the arrangement of free and fair elections. It was all pretty pointless, and served only to give the sponsors the impression that there was a degree of unity among the groups. The intention was to have all ethnic, tribal and religious groups equitably represented. Each delegate was given a voting form on which he or she (but probably a he) would vote for who should fill the assorted phantom vacancies.

The voting slips were collected. When the results were announced it immediately became obvious to me that the makeup of the opposition was not the one we had voted for. If this was not the case, then practically everyone I had spoken to must have been lying about their political leanings. I had in my mind a good impression of the political centre of gravity but the results all seemed too perfect, too West-friendly. The CIA had, it turned out, been monitoring the whole conference (which was meant to be confidential) from other rooms in the building and it is obvious that they had pre-planned the composition of the opposition long before any meaningless vote had taken place. And in a secret ballot, who could challenge the result? I felt like

I had wasted three days.

"This is bullshit!" I screamed, proving that my detectors had some use left in them. The room went quiet except for the receding echo of my yell. Everyone looked at me. I would have felt like Spartacus had a single other person voiced agreement. But I had no allies here; nobody was paying me to take a certain position. "We are here to depose Saddam Hussein and replace him with another dictatorship, are we? Fuck the CIA! They picked these names. I don't want to work for the CIA. I don't want to spy against my country!"

People standing close to me started to calm me down, reminding me that the conference was being funded by America.

"Well fuck America!" I shouted, and stormed out of the conference.

The next day I was paid a visit by someone from the CIA.

"Latif," the anonymous man said, "what do you want from life?"

"I just want to go back to my country after Saddam has gone," I replied.

"But you're not prepared to help get rid of him? Let me tell you, with your help, and the help of good Iraqi citizens like you, we want to kick Saddam Hussein from power. You alone can't do that." His tone was patronising, as though he were telling a child why not having a bar of chocolate today would be good for his teeth in years to come.

"I know that," I replied, "I'm not Arnold Schwarzenegger. I can't jump from place to place and confront Saddam, and then just kick his ass." I thought it might get through to him if I were to speak his language.

"Yes," he laughed. "One hand can't clap." He paused for a few moments. "Look, we need each other. We can supply you with whatever you want – money, weapons, protection, anything. We can have you installed in the country to start forming opposition, and when all the groups coordinate, we can easily crush the regime."

"But I have no connections in Iraq," I told him. "Just like all the others at the conference."

"We're aware of that," he said. "But we give them money, and when you have money you can buy connections – and support." I was not sure how much this awareness was exaggerated. I am sure he thought that the parties had at least a degree of support on which to build, when in fact they would be starting from scratch.

"So you want me to be your agent," I concluded.

"Why do you put it that way?" he asked. "Why don't you say, 'You want me to help my country and overthrow Saddam'?"

"I don't believe you have ever wanted Saddam gone," I replied. "You know as well as I do that you supplied him and you supported him. Now you want him gone you're just going to pay someone to get rid of him, just like you did in Egypt." Everyone has seen the film of Donald Rumsfeld shaking hands with Saddam in 1983 when the former was President Reagan's special envoy, and the US was officially neutral. It is generally understood that America backed, and tacitly instigated, Iraq in its war with Iran, mainly in order to prevent an enormous Shia bloc spreading across the oil-rich region of the Middle East; were this region dominated by Ayatollah Khomeini and his like, it would not have served the West's economic or strategic purposes. Another fact, which the world learnt about more recently, was that at the end of the first Gulf War in 1991 (which left Saddam in power), America had promised support to any group that would create an uprising to overthrow the wounded regime. An uprising was indeed sparked after such promises, and it came almost exclusively from Shia militias; America reneged on its word, and allowed Saddam's Republican Guard and Fedayeen to suppress the attempted coup. Retribution was harsh; in three days, 45,000 rebels and suspected rebels were killed by the regime, and never again was such an attempt at overthrowing Saddam made. It also left a vile taste in the mouths of anti-Saddam Iraqis. Once the nature of those rebelling was looked into, and it was found to be too close to Iran and too left-wing, the Americans simply left them to their fate. The US would only support a rebellion which would result in a "friendly" regime coming to power, so Saddam won the day. Better the devil you know. Perhaps the man from the CIA was thinking along the same lines. "That was the past," he sighed. "The world is different now. We have a plan that will return power to the Iraqi people. You can be part of it."

"And I still don't trust you," I snapped, "and I don't want to work for you or do anything for you. It goes against my nature. I never asked to become Uday's *fiday*. I always wanted a normal life. Saddam and Uday stole the chance from me and I am not about to voluntarily become part of a movement that will make such demands on me. Don't you think I have suffered enough? And I will not hurt the people of Iraq – only the regime."

"Just think about it," he suggested, as though my entrenched views were negotiable.

"I won't work for you," I asserted.

He started to get impatient and angry. His face turned red. "Latif, just as we got you out of Iraq, we could take you back there. Maybe that will persuade you."

"Fuck you," I said, calmly. "And get out of my house. We'll see how you go about sending me back to Iraq."

The threats had started. I was to become used to them.

As seems to be a tiring and repetitive aspect of my life, I found myself needing a way of saving my skin, of assuring that I could not be simply spirited away without anyone noticing. America's covert power is as potent as its B52s and aircraft carriers – and almost as subtle. They could do with me as they desired and we both knew it.

Nusa and I sat down for an important talk. I put it to her that now was the best time to get in touch with Juliette's photographer friend, William. If my story were to be printed in his newspaper, the world would know where I was and my disappearance would not go unnoticed. The Austrian government would be held accountable should anything unfortunate happen. For sure, it carried with it the risk that Iraqi intelligence, knowing precisely where I was, could more easily neutralise me. I was not being driven by a hunger for fame and fortune, either; my anonymity was useful, even vital, to me. And besides, back then I had no idea of the sums of money that could be involved in a scoop such as the one reposing in my head. I did have an idea that any publicity could help to get Nusa's daughter brought over here, and as we discussed all the pros and cons, the only possible conclusion surfaced.

A meeting was arranged with Juliette and William.

The four of us met a few days later and got settled around a table at our house in a room with coffee on tap, in preparation for a long, revealing day.

After the formalities were over, and when I had made sure that all present swore never to reveal what was about to be said, I got to the point: "I was Uday Saddam Hussein's double, and I want to have my story published." William was dumbfounded while he took in the implications of my admission. Tellingly, Juliette seemed to take the announcement calmly, which at the time confirmed to me what I had always suspected – that she already knew. She had done a reasonable job of hiding her knowledge from me, but she could never take back the look she gave me when we first met in the café where she worked.

"Please, Latif," William said, "do not tell this story to anyone. But if you will allow me, I would like to talk about this with my girlfriend." His "girlfriend" was not just anyone – she was the editor of a newspaper, and she employed him as a photographer despite his possessing no obvious talent in the field ¬– I guess I can only assume this; it's just that I never once saw him with a camera, which would be like a journalist going about without a notepad and pen.

"Okay," I said. "Ring her."

He phoned his girlfriend/editor and about an hour later she arrived at our house, slightly dishevelled, as though she had been doing something else when her phone rang. I was surprised to see that she was about sixty years old, although I must admit it never crossed my mind that to be the editor of a large newspaper does require a certain maturity. William must have had a thing for the older woman – or Austrian citizenship. It is not for me to say.

"May I introduce Senta to you," said William. We shook hands.

Over the next few hours I gave Senta a summary of my life, and watched her shift between strained concentration and disbelief as its meandering path was laid down. She must have heard a thousand intriguing stories in her time, so I was gratified to see that mine must have ranked among them. It was important, since Nusa's child was in danger, that her story, indeed her very existence in my life, was left out completely; however, we felt we had to let Senta know what was going on, in the understanding that nothing of Nusa's life would be made public. When I at last finished, silence descended on the room; we all looked at one another and tried to remain businesslike, although we each hid a little excitement at what was going on. Senta became deep in thought as she let the story resonate around her mind, and wondered what she could do with it. She at last looked up at me and said, "Latif, I don't think we can publish this story. Please, just leave this story alone, at least for now." This was not the reaction Nusa had been expecting; she burst into tears, wailing about this being the only chance of getting to see her daughter again.

I was taken to one side by Senta. "Look," she said, "here in the West, nothing comes for free. I'm not sure if I could do your story justice with our newspaper's budget. And that's the truth. You have a great story, and I'm sure someone would pay good money for it."

I asked what she meant. At that time I knew very little about publishing, and nothing about the sums of money that could change hands. As far as I knew, things like that did not go on in Iraq, where the state owned the press and competition between newspapers was not such a big deal.

She continued, "We could come to an arrangement. I could act as your agent, and we could try to sell your story to a major newspaper. With the money you could make moves towards getting your daughter out of Iraq."

The meeting ended and Senta promised to get working on my story straight away. She and William left us at the doorway.

For two weeks we heard nothing. I started to think she had forgotten about the story, or that she had changed her mind. I trusted her enough to assume that she had not simply sold my story. Besides, I had kept back several key parts, so she would not have got the whole story. I could not imagine her betraying me to the authorities. I could not imagine a Western journalist doing this, especially with what now seemed to be a big story in her possession. More worryingly, however, was the fact that I was still officially invisible. Every passing day was another opportunity for someone with power to make me disappear, and few people would be aware that I had even been here in the first place.

At the end of the fortnight's wait, however, we were greeted with what appeared to be good news; Senta had found a journalist willing to take the job on. Moreover, the newspaper he wrote for was about to launch a new magazine called News, and the editor wanted to put my story in the first edition.

"Would you be prepared to meet the journalist?" she asked.
"Of course," I replied.

The meeting took place the next day; Senta, the journalist and I were present. It was my first meeting with Karl Wendl, a tall, professional man with a deal to talk about.

"I am very interested in your story," he announced, " and I want to buy it from you."

"Buy … paying … payment," I admitted, shaking my head. "These are things I know nothing about."

Senta stepped in. "Let me deal with all that. I'm your agent, don't forget. I'll sort out a good deal for all of us."

Karl put his cards on the table: "I want to pay a hundred thousand schillings," he said. This was a large amount to me – about half the value of a house in Austria at the time, or one standard bribe from the US embassy. I had had no idea my story was this valuable. Naturally I agreed. It was an amount with which I could pull enough strings to get Tara removed from Karbala.

Two days later Karl returned with a contract. The story was to be serialised over the first three weeks of the News's existence. I cared little for such details. All I wanted was for the story to be made public. "Run it for a day, run it for three weeks – I don't care. Just pay me the money and do what you want to do with the story." Karl must have been pleased to hear this. In my artless way I was displaying a lack of understanding of the publishing industry, of journalism and of contract-making that I would later regret. The wheels were in motion, and I would soon become a recognisable face in the crowd, for better or for worse. Latif Yahia was on the verge of a kind of fame unlike the curious anonymous distinction that I had endured in Uday's employ.

I hoped desperately that the advantages would make the disadvantages worthwhile.

But I was committed now. The consequences could be dire or hugely beneficial. I was rolling a ball into a roulette wheel with no idea of the outcome.

Saddam Hussein and Yasser Araffat in Baghdad

- Chapter 3 -
Unexpected Attention

Soon after making the agreement with Karl, a new worry preoccupied me. The protecting camouflage that comes from being part of a bustling and cosmopolitan city is not, it turns out, something that comes naturally. It apparently needs constant maintenance if it is not to wear away and leave one conspicuous and vulnerable. Whether I had let my guard down during my period of settling into Viennese life or whether I had been betrayed by someone close to me was at the time a mystery, but the terrifying effect was the same: I was no longer a person in control of my own anonymity, and confirmation came in the shape of my first death threat from the Iraqi embassy.

I should not have been surprised that Iraq would stoop to issuing such threats to me and my family. In fact, after seeing what the regime was capable of doing to dissenters *without* a threat, it seemed perversely courteous. Maybe I was for some reason worth more to them alive than dead. But one day I answered my telephone to hear an Arabic voice warn me that unless I returned to Baghdad I and all of my family would be tortured and killed. The threat probably came from the top. It was well known that Tariq Aziz, the deputy president of Iraq, had a brother who lived in Vienna and had an Austrian passport, and that he had not distanced himself from the regime. It would not have been prohibitively difficult for Saddam or Uday to get such a message to me, or indeed to carry out the threatened acts. My mind had not changed, though. Being alive in Vienna was probably keeping my family alive. If they were to be harmed, any chances of my compliance would disappear. I suppose also that being threatened by Iraqis was something that I had grown somewhat accustomed to, and so I decided to carry on with my life as though the threat had never come. Perhaps it would be more truthful to say that my life carried on with slightly more suspicion, more glances over my shoulder and a reluctance to make new acquaintances. My sense of security had been ratcheted up a little rather than being sent into red alert.

If the threats were designed to keep me quiet, they failed; in fact, the exact opposite was the case. My plans to publish were given more urgency by the additional pressure put upon me. It was becoming imperative that my story became known.

Karl put his job on hold and I sat down with him and started to talk, to try to put into words the story that had been steadily growing inside my head for years. As the sentences gushed from my hitherto silent lips, he recorded me, took notes, and tapped away on a computer. Hours would slide away as pages and reels of words were recorded. I found the whole thing rather liberating, as though my mind was becoming noticeably lighter and freer. At the same time, I realised that I was taking an irreversible step into the unknown, that the story, my secret, was about to belong to the whole country and, in time, the world. And that the consequences, if I had miscalculated the risks, could be disastrous.

We worked together like this day and night for just under a week. When my work was finished he went away to put his notes into words and to come up with a story suitable to be published. He came to me one day with some rather unexpected news. The new magazine had investors who were prepared to pay substantially more for my story than had first been mooted – a figure of one million schillings, although I would still see only a tenth of this amount. In addition, the story would be serialised over three weeks. As part of the agreement, Karl would be the editor; but something was making him decidedly nervous.

"Latif," he said after he had announced the figure, "for God's sake, tell me now if everything you have said is true. If your story is not true, we will be fucked! The million will be gone, and I will be in the shit." We laughed, I devilishly, he nervously. But who can blame him for being slightly uneasy, especially given the fact that he had made such a large professional commitment to the work? It was at this moment that I realised how much he was relying on my story to give his career a boost into a higher league and to launch the new magazine with a huge, human story.

His face at last took on a serious air as he continued, "But if this story is true, then *News* will be the biggest selling magazine in Austria." (He was right – News now outsells all other magazines in the country.) He begged me for proof that my story was as I had said. I showed him documents, photographs and such like and he became visibly relaxed – and allowed himself to become excited.

Advertisements for the new magazine were placed in newspapers and bus shelters and shown on national television, with my story given as the main feature. It was then that I discovered that my story was not going to be tucked away on some inside page, but that it was to be the cover story and the first instalment of the story itself was to take up a further six pages inside. On the day of publication, a hundred thousand copies were published and within two hours they were sold out. A second run was ordered. Karl phoned to congratulate me; I could sense the exhilaration in his voice. I could not sit still, and spent the day pacing around the house. The feature had been damning to Uday, Saddam and the regime in general. How would the embassy react? Uday would soon hear about the story, and he would surely take it as my opening salvo in some sort of war. But on the other hand, I was now a recognized person myself, which could make it harder for him to harm me without being implicated himself. I feared for my family in Iraq, however; I had put them at risk. I only hoped that my calculations of the risk were correct. A hundred thousand schillings found its way to me from the newspaper. I had a post-publication meeting with Senta and William, where the editor subtly reminded me of the agent's fee we had discussed – 35 per cent, or 35,000 schillings. I held the money out and told her to take it.

"What about me?" ventured William, who had brought us together in the first place . "Here's the money," I said, holding the remaining 65,000 schillings out towards him, "take what you want." It appeared that he had not had a figure in his head, and took 5,000 schillings, which I found reasonable for the service he had given. I was left with a still-healthy 60,000 schillings. With all present, I made a vow: "I swear to God I won't take a schilling of this money. I will spend it entirely on getting Tara out of Iraq. I won't buy so much as a cigarette with it."

Later on, true to my word, I gave the 60,000 schillings to Nusa. "Here, take this," I said. "But don't forget that I sold myself to get your daughter back. I can never go back to how I was, so make sure you spend it well." I was, I thought, through with her now. As far as I was concerned I was closing a bank account or settling a debt, even though I felt I owed her nothing. If she squandered the cash it was her problem – I would not be bailing her out again. The tantrums and the calls to the police were, I dared to imagine, behind me.

Financially, I did not see the donation to Nusa's cause as much of a sacrifice. The payments I was receiving from Kessler covered my needs as an asylum seeker, particularly since we lived such a simple life, keeping extravagances to a minimum, and since we paid no rent as the house was paid for by the government. The sacrifice had been of my anonymity, and I never thought I could hold onto that for ever.

Senta seemed to be a person we could trust to begin the process of retrieving Tara, and so we approached her with a plea to help us locate – and relocate – her as soon as possible. She did not let us down. The following day she contacted the Austrian Red Cross in Vienna, who asked to see a copy of the magazine with my story in it as some kind of proof of our story. They saw our case – or rather Tara's – as worthy of immediate action and straight away set up a line of communication with the Red Cross's Jordan office. The Red Cross were at the time banned from Iraqi soil. They could arrange transport for Tara from Jordan to Austria, but we would need another way of getting her to the Jordanian border, a distance of about 300 miles by the most direct route. Nusa took this revelation as another blow. After much sighing and heavy consideration, I decided to contact an old friend who lived in Jordan. He needed some persuading that it was indeed me calling, so long had it been since we last made contact. I offered him whatever he wanted – financial or otherwise – to travel to Karbala, find Tara and take her back to

Jordan, if necessary posing as her father to get past checkpoints. Like a true friend he agreed, turning down any payment. It is not hard to imagine how moved I was by his gesture.

Two days later my phone rang. It was my friend, with a somewhat unsettling story. He said he had made it to Karbala, located Tara's grandfather and told him of the situation. He offered Nusa's father a chance of a better life for his granddaughter and in addition an escape from the threat that was looming and ready to turn devastatingly real should her presence be discovered. He refused to give her up. It would be wrong, however, to think that this refusal was down to some kind of attachment to Tara; he told my friend that if he was to come back with 5,000 dollars, she would be handed over.

Nusa took the news as I expected she would ("Fuck him, fuck my father …") but we of course had the wherewithal to see that the deal was done, a fact that must have been unexpected to her father. I wired the money to Jordan and my friend acquired the dollars. He set off again on the journey to Karbala. There was no such rebuff this time. Nusa's father's demands were met so readily that it crossed my mind how much he must be have punished himself for not doubling his ransom. With Tara declared as his daughter, my friend left Iraq and made it past all the checkpoints. It was a brave and dangerous operation and Nusa and I will forever be in his debt. As for her father, I understand that he might have been living in relative poverty, and that the payment could in some way have counted as reimbursement for any trouble or expense caused by his looking after Tara, but his readiness to seek profit from a position such as this hardly endeared him to me. I accept that I am possibly misjudging him, but I wonder whether the type of upbringing he must have given to Nusa influenced her choice of career and instilled in her a grasping, selfish attitude later in life.

Tara was taken straight to the Austrian embassy in Jordan. Shortly after, the ambassador called us and gave us the thrilling news that Tara was at that very moment in his home with his own children. He let it be known, however, that although she was safe it would be our responsibility to complete the relocation. But we were in no doubt that the most difficult part of her journey was now complete.

Senta, another of the people we were proud to have known, again got in touch with the Red Cross, and they, through the United Nations, arranged a single-journey passport like the one we had been issued with several months earlier.

Global politics being what they are, this was not going to be as straightforward as it might have been. The Jordanian regime had long been a friend of Saddam Hussein. The country also had strong historical links with the West, particularly Britain, and regularly acted as a go-between or a messenger when negotiations were deemed to be the best way of coping with a delicate diplomatic situation, but when neither side would face the other. In the West this was presented as a marriage of convenience, as though the Iraqi regime would only talk to another Arab state, and Jordan, as a neighbour, fitted the bill. Like Iraq, Jordan did have many aspects of its constitution that garner sympathy with Western sentimentality, although it is far from being a democracy. The fact that the mother of King Abdullah was British helped relations, in an arrangement reminiscent of the way kings and princesses of two powers have for millennia cemented international alliances by marriage.

The truth behind Jordan's relationship with Iraq would be much less palatable to Western minds. Jordan was, actively supporting Saddam to the point of propping him up, with reciprocal advantages in the shape of oil, dollars and strategic considerations. And as far as the government in Amman was concerned, any obvious support for the West could irritate the relationship with Iraq, which by now was irreconcilably opposed to Israel, most of the West and a US-dominated United Nations.

Ignorant of the needs of a confused and frightened little girl, the Jordanian government refused to grant me a visa to go and collect Tara. The fact was that I was openly opposed to Saddam, and could not be seen to be doing deals with Jordan that would benefit me, at least without the Iraqi regime's permission (which surely would not have been granted). Anyway, it would have been foolish for me to go to collect Tara, as agents of Saddam's regime are active and welcome in Jordan and my kidnap would have been practically inevitable without official protection.

Senta once again came to the rescue, and suggested that one of her workers pick up Tara and fly home with her. The tickets would come to about eight hundred dollars; by that time we had about a thousand left.

On 9 March 1993 – Tara's birthday, and exactly one year after Nusa and I landed on Austrian soil – the makeshift family was completed when Tara arrived in Vienna. My vow was minutes away from being delivered, and Nusa and I would soon be able to go our separate ways once and for all. I was accompanied at the airport by Nusa, Senta and representatives of the Red Cross.

I set eyes on Tara for the first time, and when the fragile three-year-old made her faltering, hurried way towards me shouting "Baba! Baba! [Daddy! Daddy!]" I was unable to resist her innocence, and experienced an instant, unexpected flush of love for her that completely disarmed me in a way that might have been expected only if she had indeed been my own daughter. How could I turn this little girl away? From that moment I was a father, and without hesitation I accepted Tara as my own. We kissed and hugged just like any parent would, but she did not seem to have any recognition of Nusa, which I found disturbing and immensely saddening. Just how long had she spent away from her over the course of her short life?

Coincidentally, it was Tara's birthday, and we had arranged a small birthday-cum-welcome party for her back at the house. The poor girl seemed so happy, so blessedly unaware of everything, of the way she was brought into the world and of the lives that had been led by her mother and "father", that it was impossible to be an impassionate observer. All present were from time to time seen to be wiping tears from their eyes.

Still, I had to move on, and so did Nusa. After the party I told her that now she was reunited with Tara we no longer needed to keep up this charade of being happily married and that we ought to start looking for separation. "That's it," I said. "I've fulfilled my promise to you."

After the troubles she had caused, Nusa's reconciliatory mood was a welcome development. "I don't know how to thank you," she said. "Anything you want, anything. I'll give you my life, anything."

"I don't want your life," I replied. "All I want is for you to be quiet. You can't talk to anyone about us." Did I trust her to give me at least this assurance? Not really, but at least I had made sure she knew the boundaries of what was acceptable to me, and could expect no help whatsoever in future were she to take a step over to the other side.

We did not split up as such; we remained in the same house and to a degree enjoyed each other's company, albeit limited by our new understanding. Tara's return had had an understandably settling effect on Nusa and she had become much more charming and sociable. I bought a Mercedes 190, a modest car, but we considered it essential for a young couple with a small child living in a busy city – especially a family that might need to make the occasional fast exit.

*   *   *   *   *

March ended, and I was given a reminder of the danger I was in. It was the third and final week of the serialisation of my story in News magazine. I had been to a restaurant with Nusa and we were leaving at half past one in the morning.

We were making our way back to the car when I heard my name being called from behind me: *"Latif!"*

Without thinking I turned round and heard two gunshots punching through the air. My training whipped itself from the dusty recesses of my brain and I pushed Nusa out of the way into the car and leapt in after her. I felt a sharp stinging in my right foot but had no time to look down before wheel-spinning off to safety. In my mirror I saw the would-be assassin running in the opposite direction. Perhaps he could have done with a few more sessions in the firing range, I thought. Or had it just been a warning? Whatever, he had hit me in my foot and lower leg, although fortunately the injuries were little more than skin lesions. Within seconds the police had materialised and I actually saw them arresting the gunman as he tried to flee. I remember saying to Nusa, "The game has started. This was the work of the Iraqi embassy." I stopped the car and was taken by ambulance to hospital.

Nusa made a return to form, and started blaming me for everything, paying particular attention to the fact that I had published my story and thereby relinquished my anonymity. I could not believe what I was hearing. "What? If I hadn't done the story, Tara would not be here," I reminded her, fighting my exasperation. "We don't have any money."

She went on complaining, pleading with me to tell her what we could do. Her selfishness was astounding, and made her father look like an angel in comparison. I was no more a friend to her than were her previous employers – a means to an end; a temporary measure. I never completely trusted her, but I always knew that deep inside her must have been a reasonable and humane soul. After this outburst I could see no point in trying to dig deep enough to reveal it.

The police were swarming around the hospital in an effort to ensure that the media did not catch wind of the latest – and nearly the last – instalment of my story. I was told at this point that the man they had captured was a Palestinian, a known member of a pro-Arafat group. Were all these agencies working hand in hand? What did my struggle have to do with his? The answer, of course, was nothing. He was probably an unprofessional hitman, who would kill his own mother for a couple of thousand dollars. Arafat himself was a prominent supporter of Iraq during the first Gulf War, although he was later to "apologise" for his stance. Right up until the end of his rule, Saddam used to reward the families of Palestinian suicide bombers financially. I could not rule out any motivation for the attempt. My stay in hospital was less than two hours long; all that was required was a little patching up. Compared to the torture I had endured in Iraq, my injuries were negligible, although the shock – albeit devoid of surprise – lasted longer.

On arriving home I straight away contacted Karl to tell him of what had happened. His response took me aback: "I've been warned by the government not to print any more stories about you for security reasons." It was obvious that this position was not open to discussion, and that his newspaper would not be running this story.

"Are you sure it's not because Iraq is such a powerful force in this country?" I put to him.

He seemed to brush the comment aside, either through ignorance or conditioning. "Whatever," he said. "Look, I'm sorry about what has happened to you, but I can't defy my paper. It looks like this story will have to be kept quiet."

We left it at that. The story remained unprinted.

*　*　*　*　*

A stagnant, debilitating mood had settled within me. I knew I was going nowhere and that any hope of progress would be dependent upon my getting back on my feet, literally as well as figuratively. In Iraq, living Uday's life, I had had available to me all that money could buy, and treats in the shape of luxurious goods and foods and exotic women from all over the world that were paid to ensure I was happy enough to feel no inclination to defy my paymasters. However, it would be wrong to say that I was by any means from an impoverished family. My father was a successful businessman, and I had graduated with a good degree in law and would undoubtedly have followed in his footsteps, either on my own or as part of his business; I would also have made a valuable employee in a contact-dependent country such as Iraq. The frivolities of life under Uday's wing would surely not have featured in any aspirations. I would have hoped that by now I would have had a wife, even children, and I would be bringing them up to lead a respectable, enjoyable and rewarding life.

All this potential had been stolen from me. My time with Baghdad's elite had been nothing but a visit to a particularly distasteful art exhibition. I owned nothing but my body, and even that had been on a time-share basis. If anything, I had been a slave, and the lifestyle I had been granted was merely part of the illusion necessary for my continued usefulness.

If I was to get even part of what was my birthright, I would have to contact my father, a move that would be burdened with secrecy and danger. Perhaps "birthright" is too presumptuous; what I needed was to reassume the flight path I had been forced to veer from when the storm hit. Our last meeting had been painful for both of us. Knowing I was under observation by Iraqi intelligence, and using Uday's disgusting persona as a way of making the spies believe I was an indoctrinated, converted member of his clan and not some disgruntled dissenter, I had been openly disrespectful and brusque with my family. The unbecoming swagger with which I had rolled out of their lives would be seared into their minds as the image of their ungrateful, detached son. An enormous hurdle had to be crossed. Would my father disown me? Would he assume I was dead? I was sure he would understand the motivation behind my demeanour – he was an intelligent man and by one action or another had for most of his adult life publicly given the impression of being someone who had never entertained so much as a bad thought about the ruling clan in Baghdad. He had no doubt play-acted his way through many an official transaction, bowing to and saluting the right people in order not to blow on the kindling of suspicion that every official must have had of every citizen. Everybody did it, and people had even done it to me when they thought they were in the presence of Uday. I could always see right through it as I needed to do it myself. I always wondered if Uday and Saddam could sense that the fawning they received from everyone they met was genuine; since they rarely experienced any other treatment, I expect they could not.

The more I thought about my plight, the more I became beset with bitterness, and was sure that my father must have been too. I hardly knew my father after reaching manhood. Saddam's war and his son's likeness to me had conspired to keep him and me apart for the best part of my adult life. The relationship between father and son is complete only when manhood arrives. The good father will take pride in his offspring's successes, his independence; they are signs of a job well done. But when the son is in need, that same pride manifests itself in a different way, in the unflinching desire to help. I had to reach him, no matter how dangerous it was.

I resolved that day to make contact with my father. It was not as difficult as I had imagined, although there was always the knowledge that unwanted parties were listening in. Whatever it was that I said, and whether or not he understood me, it worked. His fatherly spirit calmly assuaged my torment. He helped me out in the only way he possibly could – financially. He dutifully agreed to smuggle 125,000 dollars out of Iraq and into my care, although its arrival into my bank account was far from certain. I would have a long, uncertain wait ahead of me.

Nusa and I decided to find a new home. Moving targets, after all, require a steadier hand. I could afford a better place in a more amenable area of town, a large apartment where a family could settle and live in comfort. Besides, my whereabouts were without doubt being monitored by the Iraqi secret services. Perhaps they were biding their time, working out whether I was part of a network and gathering intelligence about me before they finished me off.

* * * * *

It was about this time that a second wind of interest in my story started to stir, particularly from German media. My experiences of German people, government and media had previously been somewhat limited, so I knew little of what to expect from the country. It did not take me long to discover that they are a people with whom I felt a certain affinity; ten years later my opinions on Germans have not changed – I look forward to my trips there more than I do to any other country. They are politically aware and consci-entious, and the stigma they have lived with since 1914 is undeserved; since the population has become informed and allowed to elect its own governments, they have rarely put a foot wrong.

The news of the German interest in my story was delivered to me by Karl Wendl, the editor of my story's serialisation in News magazine. He had many contacts in the country and asked if I would be interested in doing some television interviews there. Fortunately, I had recently received my Austrian passport and I was eager to take it for a test-flight. I was beginning to get used to the idea that people in Europe might be interested in my story, and Iraqi issues in general – an idea that had never struck me in the isolated environment of Saddam's palaces. I told Karl that I would gladly be interviewed on German television, and the next day, 13 June 1993, I was flown with bodyguards to my appointment with Germany's Primera satellite channel. I was looked after, put up in a five-star hotel, and pretty much treated like a celebrity or a politician; perhaps at that point I was indeed somewhere between the two as far as my public profile was concerned. I was certainly a curiosity, just like any survivor or escapee becomes. There might be something in the human condition that craves stories of endurance or bloody-mindedness, something that we all hope we can fall back on should the foundations of our comfortable lives be unexpectedly undermined. But I made sure that in every public appearance I made I steered the proceedings away from the freak show and towards enlightening the world as to what was going on in Iraq and right under their noses in Europe.

Without doubt the interview tested my nerves – it was going out live and would be forty-five minutes in length. It was a new challenge for me, making a public appearance as myself. My German was at best basic and so the entire interview was carried out through an interpreter.

Rather than when my story was published in *News*, I consider this the time when my life started to make a turn for the better, to start changing positively, the time when I could make my own decisions that would affect my life instead of having them made on my behalf for my own imagined good. For a while I also enjoyed the phenomenon of fame; people would recognise me in the street, stop and talk, ask me questions. I did not treat such attention as burdensome, as I had nothing to hide and no image to maintain. Simply by being myself I was able to sustain a level of interest because, without doubt, I had a story that people wanted to hear. With Iraq never far from the news headlines there was often an angle I could offer.

Latif Yahia in News magazine Austria 1993

After the *Primera* interview,I was showered with offers from television companies including *RTL,Sat-1* and a host of major news and current affairs channels. I only turned them down if I had another appointment in my diary. I never wanted to miss an opportunity to talk on air and steer Europeans away from complacency on Iraqi issues.

During this time I also received my first book offer. It was from a large German publisher. I had already written my memoirs, which could easily become a book, only they were in Arabic. They were somewhat different to the story that was published in News; there was more space to let the story come out at a natural pace and no real need to emphasise the sensational parts. In all I considered it a little more introspective. All that was required was a skilful translator and the book could be published expediently, an attractive proposition which would also help with my personal security problem, as I saw it. I bore the offer in mind.

My contact with the American embassy was particularly active at this time. Barely a day passed without them getting a message to me. They refused to leave me alone. Admittedly, some of the time their messages were helpful – possibly even life-saving – but there was a darker side, too. They would often threaten me. They were convinced that I was hiding secrets and they seemed to take exception to my public appearances. Threats on my life, withdrawal of security or even a forced return to Baghdad were common. It was classic good cop, bad cop stuff, deployed in their usual, imaginative way. They really wanted to keep tabs on my movements and actions, like the worried mother of a teenaged girl.

I refused to be intimidated. My next television appearances were used to make public what the American embassy was doing. I spoke of the constant attention, the spying, the manipulation. I thought that it might make them think twice before making contact with me.

But America was to hit back. Like a snake, the country's intelligence service hides away and lunges at the unexpecting; they use their power, influence and ubiquity to get their way, and they nearly always win in the end. I was soon to learn how they worked. Karl Wendl was at this time living next door but one to me. One day he called saying that an Austrian publisher wanted the rights to my story – for any price. As I had done with Senta, I told Karl that my knowledge of publishing was at base level. He told me to trust him and he would sort everything out.

This time the publisher, was a very small, unknown one, practically a one-man operation. The owner, however, was wealthy enough to make such offers. In addition he was so convinced that the book would fly off the shelves and bring success to his business that he saw the offer as a sure-fire investment rather than a gamble.

The next day Karl turned up at my apartment with the publisher, an elderly but active-looking man, who seemed excited at what was in store for him were I to sign a publishing contract.

"Latif," he said, "I am a small publisher. In fact I have yet to publish a book. Yours would be my first. I believe we could help each other."

"What is your offer?" I asked.

He made his offer and I listened impassively, partly because I didn't know if this was a good deal or not.

Karl looked at me in astonishment, and said, "This is the best offer you will ever have. You can't turn it down."

We shook hands on it.

After two weeks the contract arrived. It was in German Legalese and therefore undecipherable to me, despite my legal training. I had it translated and put forward my own changes to it that would need to be agreed upon. Film rights were to be mine and mine alone. Related media appearances and such like were also to be to my own benefit. I also strongly forbade republishing for another publisher, in another language or in another country without my express permission. I was always to be the third signatory in any contract concerning my book. I was glad I had spotted these lumbering lacunas; he accepted my changes straight away. I can never be sure if he was trying to pull the wool over my eyes, ignorant of my legal training, or whether his own contract making experience was reflected in his published portfolio I received my advance and put it in my newly-opened bank account. A few days later, my father's money arrived in Vienna. My financial security began to look brighter.

*   *   *   *   *

I decided to invest my money in a business importing and exporting clothing. I got myself an office and hired a secretary. Things were going well – I was learning to enjoy life again and I became aware that I was smiling more, something that might seem trivial to most but to me it was analogous to a gauge that measured happiness. My German was improving, even though it was tinged with a business-oriented dialect as I was learning it solely through talking to clients and suppliers – I did not have time for lessons about pets, genders and the future conditional tense.

Constant reminders that life was far from normal came in the shape of harassing calls from the Iraqi embassy. I changed my phone number. Half an hour later they called again. I changed it again. They called after another half hour. Someone from within my immediate circle must have been supplying them with details about me – I cannot be sure. My house was a secure place, my phone numbers kept confidential. This is typical of the Iraqi intelligence services. I had them rattled, there can be no doubt about it. Whenever a story about me was published, their attacks would intensify. They had great strength and long, probing tentacles – and did not like me squirting too much ink in their direction.

It would be no exaggeration to say that every intelligence service in the world was trying to get a bead on me. The **CIA** had been quite straightforward in their approaches. **Mossad,** the Israeli agency, used a slightly more oblique method. An approach was made to me by a film company. I met the German producer who told me that he was interested in dramatising my life for the screen. I showed initial interest but was wary of the immense publicity this could cause. Besides, I was contractually bound to refuse any film work until the book had been published, and could Uday be persuaded to play me? The next time I saw the producer he had 300,000 deutschmarks, which he placed on my table. Quite persuasive, I thought, but an alarm was beginning to sound in my head. Why should he be this interested? As we discussed the movie, I sensed by his language and his general demeanour that he was in no way connected with the film industry. If ever I dug beneath the emulsion, he went to pieces and tried to change the subject. Furthermore, he brought no papers, no documents, no preliminary agreement contracts –

just a case bulging with banknotes.

Anyone who has ever dealt with me knows that I never close the door in a person's face. Even my enemies get a listen. I am always open to opportunities, regardless of their origins. This I learnt from my father. It was an ethos derived from the idea that you should keep your friends close and your enemies closer – you are more likely to find out what dish they are cooking for you. I continued to meet with this eager bidder whenever he approached me, even after I had stopped believing his ostensible aims.

The film producer determined to win me over. He tried to become a close friend, and made financial offers that hinted at either a pathologic unwillingness to be rebuffed or a bottomless bank account – or perhaps too expensive a price for failure. Three times a week he visited me from Germany. He brought gifts of aftershave for me and perfume for Nusa (and other items available at all good airport terminals). My refusals continued. The more exasperated he got, the more fragrant Nusa and I became.

I was almost beginning to pity the poor guy – almost certainly a small pipe of some larger organ – when one day he approached me with an odd question: "Latif, how do you feel about Jewish people?"

"I have no problem with Jewish people or with the Jewish religion. I have no problem with Christians – or people of any religion," I replied.

"You know that ninety per cent of the world's media is owned by Jewish people, don't you?" he said. I just nodded, having no idea if this assertion was correct. "I want you to meet some film producers from Tel Aviv. Do you have a problem with Israelis?" I do not, and told him so. "These people have fabulous wealth at their disposal and could change your life. Would you meet them?"

Curiosity was biting at me, and it needed satiating. I said yes.

The meeting was arranged to take place in Germany. I made the flight and as soon as I met the people, one of them, a man of about sixty-five years of age, struck me as familiar. My memory rarely lets me down, but I could not quite put a location to the face. Where had I seen him? It was most likely on television, but certainly not at the Oscars. As the meeting progressed, my attention was blunted by my mind's activities. I was mainly travelling down blind alleys but a faint picture started to cast itself in my thoughts – the emerging image was of something to do with intelligence – Israeli intelligence. I started to think that the man with whom I was discussing film rights was one of the top people in Mossad . Sticking faithfully to his script, he promised me a green and pleasant future as the man behind the story of Uday's double, a sure-fire blockbuster if ever there was one. He was urbane, businesslike and charming. It was a shame that they were wasting their time and money on hotels, flights and entertainment for me – given the chance he could have been the next Sam Goldwyn.

The book contract was finalised. I was asked by the publisher when it could be finished and I reminded him that all it required was translation. He pointed out that after translation it would need editing for grammatical correctness and such like, and asked me if I had any objections to Karl being the editor of the project, as he had brought us together and sorted out much of the contractual work. I said as long as he was paid, I did not mind.

I sorted out the translation – a Lebanese man with perfect German did an admirable job of it. Karl and I then set about working for a whole week, going over the story, debating points, making things clearer and enhancing and softening emphasis in order to craft a paced, readable account of my life in Iraq, with Karl's valuable external, almost dispassionate, viewpoint making the story somewhat different to the one I would have had published had I been left to my own devices. In Karl's eyes, this contribution gave him a claim of co-authorship. He wanted his name on the front of the book along with mine, and intimated that that had been the understanding when we embarked upon the project. I was not so sure. It was as though he was not satisfied with the money he had already received – a considerable amount – and that he wanted a bigger cut. All I knew about editorship, authorship and ghost writing was from the Middle-Eastern model, where the originator of the story is also its intellectual rights holder, regardless of the purification it has been subjected to.

Nevertheless, it was too late now. The book was published in Austria at the beginning of August 1993 with the title *Ich war Saddams Sohn [I was Saddam's Son]*, a name I chose myself. The authors were cited as Latif Yahia and Karl Wendl. Perhaps Karl thought he was Qusay's *fiday*, although he would never have fooled me.

*   *   *   *   *

As far as my relationship with Nusa at this time was concerned, we could have been the happily married couple suggested by our passports. Indeed we had become intimately involved, and by the time the book was published she was six months pregnant with my child. I cannot really trace my transition from detesting her to impregnating her; it must have been the fact that we were sharing a dwelling and that the public affection we had to show for each other occasionally reprised in the bedroom. But happen it did. She could certainly turn on the charm when she wanted to, and be a harpy when she did not, no doubt a result of her old profession. And to say she was utterly repulsive would have been a hopeless lie; in her old profession she ranked, it must be said, among the elite.

On 4 August Nusa and I were driving to the city, inevitably passing the Iraqi Embassy. We were forced to stop near the embassy by a set of traffic lights. A car drew up along me.

A large, bearded man in the passenger seat started shouting at me: "Fuck you, fuck you!" he growled, among other things.

I rolled my window down. "Do you know me?" I asked.

I was unfortunate enough to be wearing a tie at that moment, and he jumped out of his car and reached through my window and grabbed it. Nusa let out a tinnitus-inducing shriek. In panic I punched him solidly in the face and watched his eyes roll back as he slumped unconscious onto the street. Although I was terrified both for myself and for Nusa, there was something undeniably comedic about watching this enormous brute go weak at the knees after a jab that was not the strongest in my repertoire. Some intimidating men are not used to taking punches, and I suppose he was one of them. I slammed my foot onto the accelerator and sped away, straightening my tie with my quivering hand. It looked as if I had escaped another assassination attempt, although this one must have been impromptu.

On 11 August 1993 I was having a barbecue in my garden with Nusa and Tara. It was the perfect night for it, and Nusa was under doctor's orders to eat liver as she was beginning to show signs of anaemia. I was wearing pyjamas and slippers – a decision in which no doctors were involved.

We had barely got up to temperature when in one swift, co-ordinated move, my house was sealed off in every direction except downwards. About twelve cars and a helicopter ensured that I would not make a desperate break for it, presumably threatening them with a set of barbecue tongs and a touch of cholesterol. It was Cobra, Austria's elite special forces.

"Put up your hands – no sudden moves" was screamed at me. Within seconds I was being dragged into their car and taken to the police station. I was thrown into a dank, greasy cell and left there, without a blanket and with the air conditioning turned up to its most shivering setting, and without any human contact whatsoever, until the next day.

I could only imagine that my detention was due to my continued refusal to work with Kessler, who had regularly sought my assistance with his secret services activities. I had many legitimate reasons for my refusal: I did not want to betray my country; I wanted a normal life; I had never voluntarily followed any political urges; and more recently, I did not want to put myself in any unnecessary danger since I was a de facto father and would soon be a biological one.

Kessler marched in and told me I was under arrest. I was taken to a room for questioning. I straight away recognised the interpreter they had provided for me; he was from the Iraqi embassy.

"I don't want this translator," I said. "He works for the Iraqi embassy. Get me another one."

My request was answered with a powerful slap across my face from a policeman, his eyes screwed up with hatred as he did it. I made sure he regretted his actions. Right next to me was a chair, which I picked up and with all my force hit him with it before his reactions could kick in to protect himself. He tumbled backwards with a ghostly moan of agony. In an instant the room filled with policemen, and they started laying into me and continued relentlessly. I stood no chance against so many, and got a thorough beating. No part of my body was spared; blood oozed from various wounds.

I was locked back up and had to wait until the next day before more policemen came in and took me to a prison. It was a remand prison of some sort. I was put into a single room and was not allowed a visit from friends, relatives or a lawyer. I was then informed that my bank account had been frozen. It was an outrage. Surely no one in the outside world knew where I was.

A further four days passed, still with no contact from outside. I was dragged into another interview room, where the police told me that the man I had hit – about whom I had almost forgotten – was dying, and was connected to a machine in hospital, all thanks to my actions. I started laughing. I knew how hard I had hit him, and that it was in self-defence; he was a big, strong man and there was no way I could have caused him any serious damage. It became obvious that charges were being cooked up to keep me in prison. They tried to make me sign a confession, but this was out of the question for me. Then someone said something that changed my perception of the charges against me. I was confused for a moment, but then suddenly realised that the man whom I had supposedly hospitalised was not the one I had hit with a chair in the interrogation room, but the man who had grabbed me by the tie at the traffic lights.

"I demand a solicitor," I said.

"Who is your solicitor?" I was asked.

I did not have one. I was finally allowed my call and I used it to phone Karl – my first contact with the outside world in almost a week. He spoke to the publisher and the publisher sent a solicitor. The police might have realised that I had friends in the media and that they would not be able to keep my detention a secret, especially from foreign news media.

Karl Wendl with Saddam in Baghdad 1990

The solicitor told me not to worry, saying that fighting was hardly a capital offence, indeed it was all too common, and that he would have me out of prison on bail by the end of the day. I had a good case, he told me, particularly if I had been provoked. The fact that I had been denied legal access would not show the police up in a good light.

I pleaded with him: "Look, Nusa is pregnant, they have frozen my bank account, I have no cigarettes, no clothes, and I've had no contact for five days."

He calmly stopped me. "Don't worry, I'll have you out by the end of the day.

It's all bullshit, what they say."

When he left me I was optimistic. A week later I was not. Still in prison, every day requesting the single phone call I was entitled to but being told I could not make one, I started to get desperate. I was being held contrary to basic human rights and to Austrian law, and they knew it. A further ten long, frustrating, angering prison days passed, with my conditions remaining at a level that the most egregious convicted child murderer would not have been made to endure. The door opened, and there stood Kessler. He told his guards to let him in, alone, and to close the door behind him.

"Latif," he said, sitting beside me, "I have a single question for you, and I want an answer – yes or no. Will you work with us?"

"No," I said.

"Then, Latif, I'm going to fuck you up. You'll be spending a year here – at least."

"Fuck you," I said. "What have I done to deserve a year here?"

"That doesn't matter," he said. "I guarantee you – in one year you'll still be in this cell." He had a satisfied smile on his face that made my guts tighten with loathing. He left me in the room and his footsteps reverberated along the corridor as he left.

I finally got my second meeting with my solicitor a week after this meeting with Kessler. Somebody outside the prison must have been working hard.

"I don't know what's going on," he said to me, his face grey and uncomprehending. "I've never had this much trouble before. I've applied for bail, and tried all sorts of legal means at my disposal but they just go on refusing. Did you do something else? Are the charges you've told me about the only ones?"

I swore that what I had reported to him was all I had done.

The prison eventually granted me an audience with a judge. She turned out to be a bitch like no other. Every two weeks I was allowed to apply for bail; every two weeks I was brought in front of this judge. Each time I was not even allowed to so much as open my mouth. She would dismiss me with a "no" as I was walking through the door. Is this the kind of behaviour to be expected from a country that abides by the rule of law? This disgraceful woman had no moral objections to simply sending a man back to prison without hearing what he had to say, either through a personal dislike or because of orders from above. Whichever it was, she was a long way from being suitable for any legal post, little more than a puppet, a corrupt and cowardly hand. It was beginning to feel like I was back in Iraq again, facing Iraqi reasoning and Iraqi justice. I was utterly dependent on whatever legal machinations my "team" saw fit to put in motion in the outside world, but I had no doubt that they were being blocked at every turn by people just like this judge. The idea that I would probably die in this prison started to take root. Once that has happened, the temptation to speed the conclusion on its way begins to beckon.

This went on for Two months. I was in prison when Nusa had our baby, something for which I will never forgive Austria and its diabolically jaded legal system. No doubt owing to her terror and helplessness, the triplets Nusa was carrying were delivered after only seven months' gestation. Only one child, Omar, survived, and he spent his first months in intensive care, every moment a heartbeat from death.

My publisher was feeling the strain, too. I, his big, and only, asset was behind bars at the time when he needed me out and about, attending press conferences, doing publicity and basically being there to talk to him. He put up a staggering 50,000 schillings bail – at that time the largest in the world – and was sent away.

My trial date was set for 1 October. Two days before that date, Kessler walked into my cell.

Without ceremony he started telling me what he wanted. "One. No media.

You take your book out of the market and you do it now. We will pay you whatever you ask. But you will not publish your book. There can be no word against the Iraqi government. Two. You will work with us."

I looked down at the dirty floor and gathered my thoughts for a moment. Perhaps Kessler felt a rush of victory flowing through him, the gloating euphoria of a torturer who had finally broken his victim. I looked back up at him and croaked through my dry throat, "I will be having my book published. I do not work for you. Fuck you, and fuck Saddam Hussein."

His face turned sour. "Then I repeat what I said before," he sighed, "You will stay here for one more year at least."

In that case, I thought, I have nothing to lose. In one fluid move I stood up, punched him squarely on the nose, and had the grisly satisfaction of hearing the crunching of his cartilage as it squeezed between my knuckles. He spilt nearly as much blood as I had done when his henchmen had taken exception to my assault with a chair. Holding his nose in his cupped hands, he fled from the cell, screaming.

My date with the court was not affected by my encounter with Kessler. Two days later I was taken in to face whatever charges they had brought against me. The court was held in private – no press, no jury, no observers – just me, my solicitor, a translator and the judge. The session started and the judge ordered that the man whom I had hit was summoned. He was built like an ox and towered over all around him. He tearfully related how he was close to death and that he had spent twenty-two days in hospital as a result of my punch. The time in hospital he declared was pertinent. Under Austrian law, an injury that requires a stay in hospital of over twenty-one days is deemed serious. I hoped he got bedsores waiting there, looking longingly at his calendar. I shook my head and smiled at the top of my desk – it was all a farce. He produced a doctor's report which happened to have been prepared by an Iraqi doctor connected with their embassy. The simplest inquiry could have uncovered this clumsy attempt to influence the judgement and to silence me, but the evidence was treated by the court as inarguably solid. My solicitor rejected the report, saying that only official hospital reports could be used as evidence in such cases. The judge told my solicitor to shut his mouth, and sentenced me to one year's imprisonment.

My anger boiled up again, and I leapt up toward the judge, smashing her microphone aside and thrashing at the window that separated me from justice. "One year? For what? Tell me!" I yelled, until I was restrained by a group of court officers.

I was taken away, and was this time thrown into the back of an armoured van and driven to a jail sixty kilometres outside Vienna, where I was placed in solitary confinement. Other prisoners there were three or four to a large room, with television sets and other comforts. I had a bed and a bucket, and the nauseating smell took me straight back to my first night under Uday's captivity.

My mind was a maelstrom of anger, confusion, hatred and powerlessness. I had been treated badly in Iraq but that was almost to be expected. Here I was supposed to be free, but I began to accept that I could never be free, least of all in a country with such strong links to Iraq, an officially sanctioned racism and which exercised the most vulgar form of legal arbitrariness.

It was during this internment that I developed something approaching a phobia, although with some definitions of phobia specifying an irrational fear, I am not sure if that is the correct classification for my condition. The fear was of the jangling of keys. Whenever I heard them in prison, my whole body would tense, and I would stare at the door in anticipation of it opening up and half a dozen men coming in assaulting me. They could do whatever they chose, of course, as I was practically invisible. The metallic clanking became a symbol of my powerlessness, and the god-like hold over me that the officers in general, and Kessler in particular, enjoyed. To this day that sound makes me start, even when it is I who is holding the keys. My brain is permanently wired to transport me straight back to that squalid, life-sapping black hole.

I could take no more of it. When my meal arrived I smashed the plate and with a cold, deep inhalation, slashed my wrists with a pointed shard. Death would be my only escape from this place, this situation. This was the end I had at first suspected, then foretold and was now putting into action. But there was little time for reflection; my actions this moment had been too spontaneous, and almost as soon as the blood was splattering on the floor, my cell door opened and I was bundled away to hospital.

I got no sympathy or special treatment. After a three-day stay in hospital where the bleeding was stemmed I was taken back to the same cell, again with no human contact, but this time with no access to sharp or potentially sharp objects, and no blankets or items that could be fashioned into instruments of suicide.

I thought more and more about Nusa. She had been in hospital after prematurely giving birth, and was, according to my solicitor, in a bad way. She had no money and no access to any, and I had a son whom I wanted more than anything to see, to hold. I was later to discover that she had been evicted from the apartment for non-payment of rent. She was out on the street with a newborn child and a tiny daughter in the freezing Viennese winter. Were it not for the charity of some Iranian friends who took her in, she and my family might well have died. I had been informed that I could appeal after forty-five days. They took six months to sort out my appeal. Having built up a list of reasons why I should not be held, I was transported in one of the Austrian cattle-truck police vans, but as soon as my appeal started it was dismissed by the judge, who insisted that I would serve a whole year. Again, this went against Austrian law, under which a first offence deserving of a twelve-month sentence would be considered punished after six months' imprisonment. This was my first offence, if one discounts being an Iraqi who refused to harm his compatriots. Under special circumstances the sentence might be two-thirds of the original – in my case eight months – but even this was refused. My legal team were utterly powerless. I was trucked back to my prison cell.

Every Friday a judge would visit the prison and visit every cell, asking the inmates if they needed anything and if they had any complaints about their treatment. Kessler had given strict orders that on no account must my cell door be opened to the visiting judge. The judge would have had the power to have the door opened, so there must have been a concerted effort among the staff to ensure that the judge did not see me. Whenever he visited I was taken elsewhere, hidden away.

I got half an hour's exercise per week, and spent every other moment locked in my cell. A luxury I was allowed was the ability to read the occasional newspaper. This was a valuable way to improve my German, and it at least made me feel like I was doing something positive in the wasteful drudge of daily life. I saw, heard or spoke to no other prisoner. My door remained locked constantly – I was fed through a small hole in the door which had a flap that swung open and slammed closed. I could sometimes hear the guards laughing and chatting; they would be going home after their shifts, to get on with their lives. I had nothing to laugh about. I just wanted to die. I staged three hunger strikes. One lasted thirty days, another twenty-one. My weight dropped from 105 kilograms to 66 during my stay. In September 1993, Kessler paid another visit to my cell. He made the usual offer – that I would be free if I agreed to work with him. But there was a new threat: if I refused, they would trump up some new charges and keep doing so and that I would end up spending the rest of my life there. He seemed to be enjoying this game. He felt powerful and liked to demonstrate his power. I got the feeling that if I ever did accept his offer, it would disappoint him somewhat, as it would put an stop to his power trip until the next person came along. What a despicable coward, I thought.

So I hit him harder than I had hit him the previous time, but this time I did not stop hitting him, landing punch after punch on his writhing, pathetic body until he was screaming like a baby. The guards stormed in and started to beat me into the corner of the room. This time they did a more thorough job, raining punches and batons onto my curled form, breaking my arm and inflicting agonising injuries to my entire body, the scars from which I carry to this day.

I would have given my last schilling to go back to the hell of Iraq. I would have painstakingly forged a plane ticket. That place of misery and torment became my longed-for sanctuary. It was the place of my childhood, after all. The relative security of an Iraqi middle-class childhood would not await me if I were to leave the terminal at Saddam International Airport. It would be torture, beatings, humiliation, and probably my murder. And yet my longing for Iraq never faltered. It grew with every German syllable I was forced to listen to, with every second I counted in my head waiting for human contact or death. "What if I were to be released today?" I would ask myself. "Would I go back? Could I?" Every time the mental, calculated balance tipped the same way. No. But how I wished it would one day tip the other way. I would probably move before I could change my mind. The next time Kessler's men saw me they brought news that Nusa had been seen with other men, a crude attempt to wound me psychologically. The best they could come up with was photographs of her with William, our photographer friend. This kind of treatment continued throughout my incarceration. In May 1994, Kessler came into my cell. This time there were no questions; he came simply to beat me up. I guess he was embarrassed at being given a good thrashing by an emaciated inmate; no doubt he had been telling face-saving stories to his friends and colleagues about his heroic grapple against an unprovoked attacker. He felt the need to bring an iron bar with him this time. I fought back as best I know, but was overwhelmed and beaten up badly, leaving me bloodied and broken in the corner. It was only physical pain, though. He could not penetrate me any further.

By 12 June, a new prison officer had arrived at the prison, and Kessler made a decisive mistake. He had not seen fit to tell the prison officer that I was a special case and that I should not come into contact with the judge. During his Friday visit, the judge was introduced to me. He was something of a character – he was highly respected in the field but had a serious weakness for alcohol, and lived almost all his life in a staggering haze. I was lying on my bed in my prison uniform and slippers, and in walked the judge, given access by the out-of-loop prison officer. I had no idea who he was, and must have shown it.

"I am the judge," he announced. "How is everything?"

I was less than impressed, and took off my slipper and started to slap him on the face with it.

"Are you mad?" he pleaded, trying awkwardly to dodge my attacks, "I'm a judge!"

"I don't care," I raged, "Fuck you and fuck your country."

"Why are you here?" he asked, simultaneously dodging my swipes. I suppose I would have hit him harder had he not looked so physically defenceless.

"I'm on holiday here. Why do you think? I'm a prisoner. I don't know why I'm here. I got one year for nothing."

"And how long have you been here?"

"Ten months," I replied.

"And do you have a criminal record?"

"No," I said. I smelt progress, and stopped slipper-whipping him.

"How come you weren't let out after half your time?"

"I don't know. I wasn't let out after half, and I wasn't let out after two-thirds."

"If this is true," he said, "then you will be released today. You will come with me." We went to the prison office and discovered that there was no file on me. As far as the prison's officialdom was concerned, I barely existed. "What is your name?"

"Latif Yahia."

He started tapping into a computer. Nothing came up. He started to scratch his head. The officers looked at each other, their faces contorted with horror and embarrassment. "Who opened the cell?" they were heard to whisper to one another. The new officer innocently admitted that he had opened it.

They told him he had been instructed not to, but of course he denied it.

The judge became impatient. "Where is this man's file?" he said with a raised voice.

One of the officers had to admit that I had been brought in by the secret services and that there had been instructions not to let my presence be known.

"What?" shouted the enraged judge. "This is Austria, not some backward country, not a dictatorship! Where is the democracy? You have all broken the law!" He picked up a form and said, "This man, he will be released now." The guards froze as their brains tried to make sense of their conflicting thoughts. Did at least one of them consider for an instant throwing the judge into a cell to keep him quiet until Kessler arrived? It would not have surprised me; that seemed to be the mindset around here.

Naturally I was elated, but I had to face a reality of my own. I said to the judge, "Sir, I don't want to be released. As soon as I'm free I'll be re-arrested and thrown back in prison."

"Latif," he replied, "You are now in Austria. It's not that kind of place, you know. We can't just throw people into prison for no reason. We have laws here – laws against exactly this kind of behaviour. I can guarantee that you will not be sent back to prison." As he spoke, he was shaking his head in disbelief. Everything he had studied for, devoted his professional life to – the law – was being abused and overlooked as though it were one of several options open to the state when it came to dealing with specific issues such as mine, rather than being the basis of the country's democratic status that was both its foundation and its overarching principle.

He asked me where I lived. I told him that I lived in Vienna, but that I could not be sure that my wife and children would still be there. "Where are your clothes?" He asked. "You are going home." All I could think about was the pyjamas and slippers I had been wearing when I was arrested at the barbecue.

He told me to wait where I was while he sorted out some details and some clothes, and one hour later he returned and drove me back to Vienna. After all the pain I had endured, the guilt and embarrassment I felt about hitting the judge with my slipper made me feel awkward. This apparently doddering man let me carry on striking him so he could hear my story, even though he must have feared for his own safety. He was braver and infinitely more gallant than all of the strapping guards combined.

During our journey I told him what had happened to me. Until then he did not even know who I was, which makes his insistence that I was released all the more remarkable. I watched his face light up as he instantly recognised me as the person he had read about in the newspapers. He pitied me and assured me that never again would I be treated like this in his country. But there was also a realisation that I was particularly vulnerable to attack and so he made sure he did not leave my side until I was safe.

The house Nusa and I had lived in was empty. We embarked upon a frantic search of the city, neither of us even knowing if anyone from my family was still alive. The judge, the only worthwhile human I had met in nearly a year, fought back tears as we toured the streets trying desperately to come up with ideas. At the same time, I continued relating my story to him, but there was now a new chapter, and the sorry events had taken place in the country he loved.

"So this is what they did to you here?" he said, solemnly.

"Yes. This is what has happened to me."

"Do you want my advice?" he said. "Leave this country. Two countries control Austria: Iraq and Iran." He went on to tell me the story of Dr Qassimlou, who was secretary-general of the opposition Kurdistan Democratic Party in Iran. The Iranian government made several attempts to assassinate him but each time they failed. He was invited to Vienna by the Austrian government in 1989 to attend a conference of Iranian opposition leaders, an offer he accepted. While he was in the country he was murdered by an Iranian assassin. The killer was caught but released and sent back to Iran in what would appear to be a pre-planned move. "Is that how you want to end up?"

"No," I said.

"Then leave the country."

Latif Yahia in Vienna with the Ambassadors of Saudi and Kuwait at an OPEC Conference, 1992

We eventually located Nusa and we were reunited. More important, I met my son for the first time. Before I was taken to prison we had had an ultrasound scan performed, so I knew the child was a boy. We had already decided to call him Omar, and at last I could hold him in my hands. It is not difficult to imagine my happiness at that moment. At length I told the judge about my frozen bank account. He rolled his eyes in exasperation and told me not to worry about it. He told me that that particular law was only applicable to terrorists. The next day the freeze was lifted.

I had been as low as it is possible to be. I had attempted suicide and been held in harsh, desensitising conditions for over ten months of my life. Even in Iraq, the torture had come at intervals and was almost expected. Here, in this free country, the torture and the physical and mental beating was non-stop, relentless, and I was utterly blameless .But now the world would hear about Austrian hospitality.

Charly Blecha bei Wendls Fest

Zur Präsentation kam ein weiterer Intimkenner des arabischen Raums: Als NEWS-Redakteur Karl Wendl seinen Tatsachenbericht „Ich war Saddams Sohn" vorstellte, zeigte sich Ex-Minister Karl Blecha, seit kurzem Geschäftsreisender im Vorderen Orient, begeistert. Von Öl bis zu goldenen Wasserhähnen reicht sein Handelsgut. Blecha: „Wenn ich weiß, daß die in Abu Dhabi sich Keramik-Klomuscheln mit Pfauenmuster wünschen und die in Gmunden so was produzieren, vermittle ich es."

Duett. Alt-Minister Blecha mit Buch-Autor Karl Wendl und Opus.

Ex Austrian Minister Charly Blecha at Book Launch of
"Ich War Saddam's Sohn" with Karl Wendl during Latif Yahia's
incarceration in an Austrian/ CIA prison 1994

- Chapter 4 -
Shackled by Liberty

The day after my release from prison I was visited by Karl Wendl, the editor of the feature in News. He seemed hurried and barely mentioned the fact that I had been locked up without cause for nearly a year. It turned out he wanted to talk business and had no time to waste.

"Latif," he said, "while you've been in captivity there has been an enormous amount of interest in you. TV companies, newspapers and seemingly everyone else want to talk to you. Your story has proved to be quite a hit. I think it has got inside people."

"I am ready to talk," I replied. Having been silenced for the best part of a year I had plenty to say. "But not to Austrian TV," I added. "I want foreign TV." I could see little benefit in talking to Austria from within its boundaries. It seemed like a country that had already made up its mind about most issues and was in no mood to hear any opposite views or unofficial facts. I was also sure that I, and any sympathetic media organisations, would have to jump so many hurdles that I would not be given a fair hearing, or would have to fight against the machinery of state and its powerful departments. Karl told me that I could work with a Dutch TV company called **TRUS TV**, and **RTL 2** in Germany, both of whom had been in constant touch with him, never giving up hope of getting me on their frequencies. "We could go tonight," he said.

"Let's go then," I enthused. I felt like I could not waste another second. Inside me was a turbulent, pressurised, explosive force that needed release. It was the force that had led me to the physical outbursts of the previous year, but which now had a chance of a more productive and, I hoped, more damaging outlet. I was determined to make absolutely clear what was going on in Austria, and people could make up their own minds as to whether this was behaviour becoming of a civilised European democracy. Whether the public chose to believe me or not would not be my main concern. I knew it was the truth and that was all that mattered to me. What would I have to gain from spreading falsehoods about Austria? If I were pro-Saddam I would be damaging the reputation of a valuable ally in Europe. As someone immeasurably opposed to Saddam, I would be creating danger for myself by antagonising the government in Austria, who might turn a blind eye to my ill-treatment or disappearance, just as they had done with Dr Qassimlou. After all, I was still living there and despite the judge's warnings, had no immediate plans to leave. There would be no logical reason to lie about my treatment.

My first interview was with Germany's RTL-2. In the hour that I was granted I landed blow after verbal blow on the Austrian government, detailing their illicit links, what I saw as their inherent racism, their means of justice, the mental torture, the beatings, the blackmail, the murder. I paid special attention to Austria's links with Iraq and how their Iraqi link was more than simply a means of keeping open a diplomatic gateway; it was a thriving, two-way relationship that allowed billions of dollars to move between the countries, and all this at a time when Iraq and its leadership had pariah status in the international community.

Finally being given a voice was liberating beyond compare. I had to keep reminding myself that my new-found liberty was really only as a result of the error Kessler made when he neglected to keep the guard informed of my special status. Were it not for that oversight I would still be there now, waiting for the hatch to open so I could have a bite to eat, trying to guess when my next beating would come and how severe it would be. Viewers of TRUS TV in The Netherlands were treated to further revelations, although I would later have cause to regret doing this interview thanks to the most unforeseeable of situations.

After completing the interviews and unburdening myself of some of the anger that was boiling inside me, a question dawned on me: Why was my story so popular in The Netherlands and Germany? Why was I in such demand? My story was big in Austria, but this would surely only result in limited attention elsewhere. How had the masses caught onto my story? Germany I could understand; they spoke the same language as is spoken in Austria, so it is possible that a small number of books might have blown, pollen-like, over the border. But Holland ? I confronted Karl with my concerns, half-anticipating his response. It turned out that while I was in prison, my Austrian publisher had sold the rights to my book to publishers in these two countries at least. This was, of course, contrary to the part of our contract stating that I would be a signatory of any international publishing deals. In other words, fraud.

At my next opportunity I challenged the publisher over the issue. "Why have my books been published in Germany and Holland without my signature?"

"What could I do?" he pleaded. "You were in prison."

"This is bullshit," I replied. "You broke the contract. It isn't up to you where and when my story is published."

"But you'll get paid your royalties," he reasoned.

"I know I will, plus I want my book rights back."He seemed flustered by this, and started explaining himself wildly. "I had to do it. It was the right moment – there was interest in the story. Don't you think you'll benefit from the sales? I took an executive decision. And don't worry. You'll be paid."

I had no idea of the details of the contracts he made with these countries' publishers. More important, I had no opportunity to amend or reject them. I had good reason not to trust him.

I then found out that he had signed a deal with an American publisher to publish my book in English translation under the title I Was Saddam's Son. This publisher had then gone on to publish the title in Canada and Australia. I contacted them, insisting that they withdraw the book and pay me the royalties that were owed to me, but they refused on the grounds that the book was under Karl Wendl's name and that he had been the signatory of the contract. I explained that he had no right to be the signatory, that we had our own contract which stipulated that I and I alone held the rights to the story, and that any reproduction required three signatories – one of whom was to be me. In other words, the contract they had made was null and void as it was not made with the consent of the rights owner. This, they told me, was a matter between me and him. I am not sure that they would defend this viewpoint so aggressively were I to produce an Arabic version of one of their titles posing as the owner of the work's rights. They refused to withdraw the book, and to this day have never paid me a dollar in royalties, or even given me any details of the sales figures.

In contrast, when I approached the Dutch and German publishers with the same objection, they recognised the illegality of their contracts – that they had effectively been conned by Norka – and took the book from sale immediately. However, I still received no royalties from them, as they had already paid them to Norka, and it was therefore up to me to sue them under the terms of my own contract with the publisher and Karl Wendl.

It was around this time that the owner of Norka conveniently declared himself bankrupt. He must have enormous holes in his pockets or very expensive tastes, as the proceeds from my book alone must have run into the millions. His promises to pay me "very soon" continue to this day.

The episode highlights an interesting comparison between the American and the European attitudes to intellectual property. It seems that in the US, it belongs to the publisher, whereas in Europe, or at least in The Netherlands and Germany, it stays with the author. I have tried several times to use legal means to have I Was Saddam's Son withdrawn or to receive a share of the royalties – but preferably both – but have been blocked all the way by the American system. What is more, I was forbidden from entering the country to take Arcade to court. Somebody has made a good deal of money out of me, and it would appear to be impossible to recover it.

That said, Ich war Saddams Sohn was never the complete story, as it had been censored. I was not allowed to mention my treatment at the hands of the Kurds, who kidnapped and imprisoned me on my escape from Baghdad, since anything to do with the Kurds was at that time a sensitive issue – even more than it is now. This was when the Kurds were attempting to put their differences aside and form a homogeneous and reputable opposition to Saddam in the north of Iraq, even though it was proving very difficult to give up, or at least to share, their tribal and territorial claims. Anything that portrayed the Kurdish region as being in a state of anarchistic turmoil would not have been published. I think this is called freedom of speech. Several other such issues had been cut out of the two translations of the book, and the whole, true story had to wait until the publication of *The Devil's Double* to be told.

After months in a financial coma, and with any proceeds from my book far from guaranteed, I had a pressing need to start earning some money. I restarted my import–export business, and it fortunately resumed more or less where I had left off. Before long I needed to employ a secretary, and I was lucky enough to find Sara, a capable and conscientious Austrian.

An air of normality then returned to my life, and my daily dealings kept my mind and my bank account active. I felt slightly more secure in the knowledge that the judge who had got me released from prison was keeping a close watch on my case. I only hoped he did not drink himself to death or become a victim of Austrian Iraqi justice himself, and not only for purely selfish reasons; he had become something of a friend to me and I held him in great affection.

One day a man arrived at my office asking to see Sara. I let him in and asked him to wait while I went into Sara's office to get her.

"Who is this guy?" I asked. It was odd for someone to come to see her personally rather than to see her as part of the business.

"He's my uncle," she replied.

"Ah," I said.

"He's … He's Jewish," she said, almost apologetically. This was not the first time that it had been feared that I might have harboured an uncontrollable mistrust of Jews. It was almost certainly due to the fact that I was an Arab rather than to any echoes of the Third Reich and its Austrian *Führer*. Having been mistreated by Muslims, Christians and atheists in my life, I had learnt to treat people as individuals, and their religion or lack of religion as neither justification nor explanation for their actions. "I am Jewish too," she then confessed, as though her employment was hanging in the balance. In fact, my Islamic belief does not determine my actions in a traditional sense. I come from a country whose population is chiefly Islamic but which has for decades been secular as far as the law is concerned. Alcohol, for example, was permitted in Iraq, and yes, I had drunk it many times, and still do. I think that what matters is that you lead a good life, not that you follow certain scholars' or activists 'interpretations of ancient books. Islam is really an Abrahamic denomination, just like Christianity and Judaism. It is largely a matter of luck which one you are born into, or whether you are born into any of the other world religions or into atheism. What you choose to do with that initial roll of the dice is your own business.

"It doesn't matter to me," I said. "I am a Muslim – so what? It makes no difference."

Sara's uncle must have heard the conversation, as he strolled into the office and joined in. "You don't care? But you're a Muslim!" He looked quite surprised, but throughout my life I can count on one hand the number of Muslim associates I have had who had any serious misgivings about Judaism or Jewish people simply because of their faith or ancestry, and such people were unlikely to become my friends. Perhaps this man had had some bad experiences.

"Not all Muslims hate Jews," I exclaimed. "There are Jews in the Quran, Judaism is a recognised religion. Why should I hate them?" I embraced him and guided him into my office. "So what do you do for a living?"

He said, "I'm a diamond wholesaler."

"Brilliant!" I said, in ignorance of my own pun.

"Do you know anything about diamonds?" he enquired, his ears straining so much that his eyebrows raised.

"Only enough to buy them from a jewellers," I explained. "Apart from that I don't know *anything* about them."

"Would you be interested in being involved in diamonds?" he asked me.

"How can I be involved in something I know nothing about?"

"I can teach you," he said.

I had no idea why he wanted to get me on board, particularly as I did not even have a novice's level of appreciation of his trade, but I accepted his offer. Once again my curiosity had got the better of me.

Over the following month, he came and visited me nearly every day, teaching me everything I needed to know about the diamond industry, its products, processes and politics. By the end of the instruction I knew all about grades, cuts, inclusions, sizes, carats, colours and, more importantly, about the complex business itself. I regularly expressed disbelief at the amount of work that goes into each stone in each piece in each shop. Without doubt it was a fascinating and politically charged business, and I grew eager to get started.

"You know," he said to me one day. "I think it's time you were involved in this business? Are you prepared to get going?"

"I think so," I said.

"There's more than 800 per cent profit in it."

"Then why not ?" I smiled.

"To get started you need a minimum of two or three million dollars."

I stopped smiling. I told him I could not afford it, and considered my new-found ambition vaporised.

"What if somebody helped you?" he asked, then almost in embarrassment added, "for a share in the profits, of course."

"Then yes, I'd do it," I replied. Regardless of the fact that I was still not sure exactly what this new opening would involve, I agreed to dive in.

"Well," he shrugged, "I am going to help you. Tomorrow I'm flying to New York, but in a week I'll be coming back and then we can talk." I prayed for a tail-wind on his return. I was eager to get started.

A week later he came to visit me. He had a suitcase with him. He placed the case on the table and without saying a word, opened it up. Inside there was one and a half million dollars in cash. I gave him an impressed look, but tried not to look too excited.

"Count it if you want," he said.

"I can't count all that," I replied.

"Well, it's 1.5 million dollars. I'm going to contact our agent in Nigeria and tell him who you are, how you will be arriving in the country and such like." So this African nation was to be my destination, I assumed. But I was still puzzled as to why it was me who would be the one going. He had put an enormous amount of faith in me. "How can you trust someone you have known less than two months?" I asked.

His reply was that he had heard about me, partly from Sara, and that he considered me a good guy, that I talk straight, that I do not cheat people, that I am honest. "You are the sort of person we like to deal with." I almost blushed.

"Are you sure?" I asked. I needed to know if I should write out a receipt, a contract or something.

"Latif," he said, sternly and forcefully. "I'm going to tell you something now, and I want you to keep these words in your ear like an ear-ring that won't come out. *Don't mess with us.* Diamonds are like drugs. If you try to play games, just remember, the organisation is bigger than you. Play games and they will cut your head off. Stay honest, please your boss, take your agreed cut, and you'll be safe, happy and rolling in money. Good, honest men and women are hard to find and we treat them with the respect they deserve. Be a team member and I promise you, you'll have nothing to fear. Try to go alone and you'll regret it. My own reputation is at stake here, too. But I trust you, so I am not worried. Just remember my warning."

I had made no plans to double-cross my contact, but his warning was sobering. I agreed on the spot.

I made my first trip to Nigeria with 1.5 million dollars in my suitcase. When the Twin Towers were still standing, this would hardly have raised an eyebrow, but post **11 September 2001,** an Arab, African or Asian walking around departure lounges with this much cash would have been the subject of intense suspicion and scrutiny. I needed to have false passports made for me, as some countries will not grant a visa to certain other countries. My passports were Dutch and American, which, I was told, would allow me entry to practically every country, as very few had poor relations with both of them. On the advice of Sara's uncle, I took a further precaution to avoid unnecessary attention at airports – I dressed as though I were Jewish. With my skull cap in place I was virtually assured unchallenged passage through customs in all the countries I was to visit. Anti-Jewish violence and sentiments unfortunately still exist in many parts of the world, and I find such opinions disgusting and inexcusable. But one effect – which I could use to my advantage – is that official, popular and legislative influence means that Jewish people are less likely to be randomly picked out for a customs inspection in case the inspectors should be accused of anti-Semitism. Someone like me from the Middle East can pass himself off as an Israeli with relative ease. I was at first uneasy about exploiting this political issue for personal benefit, but once I witnessed the effect my skull cap had on airport security, my misgivings diminished.

Latif Yahia with Marie Colvin of The Sunday Times in Vienna 1994

I met my African contact in Lagos, and, after a businesslike meeting, bought a batch of diamonds with the 1.5 million dollars, and within hours was on a plane soaring back to Amsterdam. Another contact was waiting for me there, and I gave him the diamonds in return for 2.5 million dollars. From then on they were out of my hands and would no doubt go on to multiply in value many times as they made their way to the window displays of Europe's elegant jewellers. A single trip had netted me a million dollars, and for several months I was making that same trip two or three times a month.

I was becoming wealthy much quicker than I had thought possible. Had my university training been put to good use, I would probably now have been a lawyer, possibly a successful one working for a large company. Any chances of that outcome had been made impossible by war, Uday and my flight. But my wealth would not even have approached what I was gathering at this time, and for much fewer hours' work – even lawyers' hours.

If only I could have shared my wealth and my knowledge with my father. He was a clever and wise man, and I missed him dearly, more than I had when I was Uday's fiday and we were forced to be apart. At least then I was in the same country, the same district as him. I frequently recalled the time when I was driving with Uday past the street in which my family lived, during an Iraqi celebration of the end of the war with Iran, when the streets were thronged with cheering people and gunfire was tearing holes in the sky. I looked down that street, just to catch a glimpse of anyone from my family. But they were not on the street firing guns with the other Baghdadis. They knew that this was no victory. What is more, they had no idea where I was, or whether the war everyone was celebrating the end of had actually claimed me as one of its countless victims. In a way, of course, it had.

In Austria I did not even have a street to peer down.

Austrian intelligence agents were not unaware of my new wealth, and redoubled their efforts to get information on me and, it seems, to make my life a misery.

I was also approached by the intelligence services of dozens of countries, including Israel and Iran, and they were offering me immense sums of money to work with them. I never took a single penny from them. I was not for sale, and financial bribes had as much chance of success as did their ideological reasoning. My rebuttal followed the same lines for each country that approached me: I could not oppose Saddam Hussein on my own. If I were to actively oppose him I would need to align myself with one of the opposition groups, and since every group is financed and supported by a particular country, be it Iran, Saudi Arabia, Kuwait, the USA or Britain, this was out of the question. This was in addition to the fact that I could never trust any of them and was convinced that personal gain was the driving force behind most of these groups' leaders, even where the followers themselves had valid and passionate reasons for joining the cause. They never seemed to understand that I was opposed to Saddam Hussein, his son and his regime, not Iraq and the Iraqi people, and that I would not support any group threatening to use invasion or terrorism to overthrow him because of the damage, injury and death that would be brought upon my country's innocent people and their livelihoods.

This letter addressed to the Republic Palace, confirms that Latif Yahia's Iraqi citizenship had been revoked after his flight and that his personal file had been destroyed. In effect wiping away his life in Iraq 1992. This letter was found after the invasion of Iraq in 2003

The Iraqi intelligence services were as predictably sinister as ever. They would often call me with threats and they were starting to harass my family back in Iraq. My mother and father were arrested, as were several other members of my family. I received phone calls from my mother from inside the offices of Iraqi secret services. They knew exactly how to get to me. These tactics caused me as much distress as had my own periods of captivity. It was the hopelessness, the lack of information, that tore up my brain. And Uday knew exactly what he was doing. He was a tyrant; that was without question. But he lacked any guile or subtlety, and his life was spent trying to please his father by pleasing himself. He would mimic his father's actions but out of context, and had on many occasions caused the family much embarrassment by his recklessness. I would tread carefully in my dealing with him, as he was always on the precipice of brutality, but I knew I could always outwit him. At the end of November 1994, I received the call I had been expecting but dreading. It was from Uday himself. "Listen to me, you bastard. Don't put the fucking phone down. I am sitting with your father and mother beside me."

"Fuck you," I snapped. "I don't believe you." Naturally I did believe him. There was nothing whatsoever to prevent him from having my father taken to his palace. My declaration gave me a few seconds to think, however, as I knew he would gloatingly prove his assertion.

"I'll let them talk to you," he sneered. There was a short pause. Thoughts ricocheted around my skull.

My father's voice, brave and dignified, came down the line. We greeted briefly, but both knew we could say nothing. He confirmed that he and my mother were there in Uday's office and that Uday wanted to talk to me. It was a heart-stopping exchange. They passed the phone back to him.

"What do you want?" I asked.

"I'm offering you amnesty," he snarled. "Just come back to Iraq."

I could not suppress my laughter. The suggestion was so ridiculous I could not even begin to believe it. "You want me to come so you can kill me," I said.

"Listen, do you want to see your father and mother alive again?"

I said yes. It was a stupid question, but I was in no mood to show contempt. "Well, I have a visa that will allow them into Thailand. I will send them there and you can go and meet them." In the background I could hear my brother, who was still a boy, screaming, "I want to go, too." Hearing him in such distress made me feel like I was being strangled with the telephone cable, and I would have screamed with pain had I not been able to call upon my last dregs of mental strength.

Uday responded. "Okay, I'll send your brother, too. But as for your other two brothers and two sisters, I will look after them." He was keeping them as hostages, this was implicit. "If your parents don't come back to Iraq, I will kill all four of them." There was arrogance in his voice, yet the very fact that he was calling me and practically begging me to return told me something important: that my sniping against him was beginning to hurt him; he was concerned for his own safety and probably would not harm my family as long as I was out of reach. Judging by what I knew of the way his mind worked, he would consider himself perfectly able to come up with a deal that would have me shaking hands with him at the airport within weeks.I said that I would accept the arrangement. "Latif," he carried on, "I'm not going to give you the details of the deal I have arranged for you. I'm not going to tell you my offer over the phone. I'm going to leave it up to your father to tell you when you meet. You don't have to agree or disagree yet."

Again I said I understood, although whatever the deal was, I was quite sure it could not possibly benefit me. Right at that moment, however, I would have agreed to almost anything just to embrace my mother and father for a single second.

"Next week they are flying from Jordan to Thailand, at my expense," he concluded. "You will have to make your own way there. Don't worry. I won't try anything."

It all sounded so familiar. "Uday," I warned, "don't play games with me." I felt that I did indeed have the weight of my knowledge on my side of the scales. He was not finished with me yet, and it did offer some protection to my family. But with people like Uday, for whom the powers of logic and rational thinking were not strong, that was no guarantee at all.

We set off en route to Thailand the next week, this time with eight Swiss-trained bodyguards, among the best in the world. Being both wealthy and in the sights of the world's intelligence agencies as well as those of the Iraqi administration, danger was all around, and I was not about to start taking chances. But I trusted my bodyguards unreservedly. They were highly professional and if they had any political, religious or national loyalties that would be of detriment to me, they did not betray them. With uncertainty spinning around our minds, Nusa, Tara, Omar, my eight bodyguards and I touched down at Bangkok International Airport.

The meeting had been arranged to take place in a hotel; our party was staying at another hotel. I sent the bodyguards ahead of me to check that everything was safe, and to get into position to clean up should anything happen. I received their security clearance and went to meet my father, mother and little brother.The surge of emotions we all felt was debilitating. This was not the meeting I had planned, but right then any meeting would have sufficed. I always had a feeling that I had voluntarily betrayed them, no matter what my intellect told me. They were intelligent people, though, wise to the way in which Saddam's rule operated; they would never have blamed me for anything that had happened or what was now happening, and I was wrong to think they would have. It was impossible to catch up on all our stories in the short time allowed by this initial meeting, and anyway we were too overcome with emotions to deal with specifics or what had now become trivialities. We just talked about nothing, or sat in silence, looking at each other's faces. There would be time to talk properly later; we had all planned to stay a few days. Did Uday suppose that a longer stay would allow me to get so close to my family that all my powers of reason, all my mistrust of him, would crumble?

My father eventually and reluctantly got round to giving me the details of Uday's deal. First, and most preferably, I would return to Iraq. This was unlikely, of course, and Uday knew it. If I did not want to go to Iraq, Uday would set me up in business anywhere in the world with his own money. I would be allowed to take fifteen per cent of the profits, and Uday himself would get the rest. It was basically a laundering operation, with a very public Saddam-hater as its director to lend it respectability and legality; Iraq was still under the grip of United Nations sanctions, and Uday's business interests were being discovered and closed down at an unmanageable rate, eating into the edges of his playboy lifestyle. I learnt that the majority of the so-called Iraqi opposition were involved in the same arrangement, although not necessarily with any duress placed on them. As long as they kept up the act that they were opposed to Saddam, indeed that they were trying actively to overthrow them, nobody would suspect them and the sanctions could effectively be circumvented. Whenever there had been an anti-Saddam conference, the details of who had said what, supposedly in private, had been faxed to Baghdad within minutes of the end of the talks. I was urged by my father not to believe the opposition and under no circumstances was I to work with them.My opinions of the oppositions had, as it happens, been formed much earlier. I was convinced that they were all criminals, fraudsters and traitors and were using Saddam's grip to boost their own fortunes, at the expense of the beleaguered populations they claimed to represent, and to the betrayal of all their hopes and dreams. Many of the politicians who miraculously rose to the surface after Saddam's overthrow were as well known to me as they were mistrusted.

We stayed in Bangkok for several days. It was exhilarating to see my parents and brother again and to catch up on practically every aspect of each other's lives. We had had so much potential time together stolen from us that every minute spent together counted for at least week apart. My mother and father met their grandson and their adopted granddaughter, and Nusa. The time was frequently spent with damp eyes as we fought the tears that tyranny wanted us to spill.

On our final day in the city, my father hugged me and kissed me for the last time. While he held me he said, "Latif, I know you are strong, and you are my son, and you know how much I hate the Iraqi government." He gripped my head and gazed into my eyes. "Don't take any offer from Uday. This is your choice, but as your father I tell you, do not take it. Don't do it for us. You are a multi-millionaire now; you don't want money. If God wants us to be alive, we will be alive. He is more powerful than Uday or Saddam. If God wants us dead, we are dead."

"Don't go back to Baghdad," I urged him, knowing as I said it that he could not possibly leave Iraq behind.

"I have to," he said. "Or your brothers and sisters will be killed. Do not doubt that."

We parted later that day. It was the last time I was to see my father. Despite a heavy, sorry, aching heart I had no choice but to return to Austria and continue with my diamond business. My father was right. By taking Uday's offer I would have been helping to prop up the regime for longer than its natural life. I have no doubts that any of my family who survived would have been subjected to more hell from the clan whatever decision I made. I was more use out of Iraq, independent of it, than inside it, another of its puppets. From outside I could use my freedom to tell the world the truth about what was going on inside the country; I had been backstage, behind the curtain of the Western media. And I had found that people in some parts of Europe were at least prepared to listen. They had an abject distrust of their governments and their motives, and since these were the very governments that were helping to keep Saddam in power, while publicly opposing him, the truth could indeed prove punishing. I was a potential instrument of that punishment, and backing down – even if I were to suspend belief and imagine that I would survive my return to the regime's grip – would be yet another missed opportunity for the Iraqi people and yet another victory for the powerful, despotic clan. It was that important.

My father's advice and my own instincts, both agreeing that we should not take Uday or Saddam up on any offered deal, were to receive reassurance about a year later. In August 1995, two of Saddam's sons-in-law, Hussein Kamel and Saddam Kamel, fled Iraq in fear of their lives. In brutality they almost equalled Uday himself, and it was believed that it was fear of Uday himself, rather than Saddam, that forced them to flee. Uday was said to have felt threatened by their presence. As well as being his brothers-in-law, they were also cousins, a relationship that was close enough to cause considerable succession headaches for Uday. They ended up finding refuge in Jordan, even though it was well known that they were brutal bullies in the Saddam mould. It is possible that they felt homesick, missed their families or were not used to roughing it in Jordan where the power they had once held would count for little. But the following spring, they started to make moves to get backing into Iraq via an official pardon. It was granted. Their initial flight was presented by the regime as an innocent error of judgement, an understandable response to the pressure they were under. They were told that they were welcome to return to Iraq and would be welcomed as brothers. The two came home to an emotional reunion, being met at the Border with all official respect. They were photographed smiling and being welcomed. It was all a front. Within hours they had been murdered by the regime, although the official story was that they had got caught up in a gunfight and had unfortunately been killed.

Was I intended to be the prototype for this manoeuvre? It is extremely likely. Had Uday been a little more shrewd throughout his life, I might have taken him up on the offer. I was, after all, desperately homesick myself. It is also likely that had I returned and been murdered, Hussein and Saddam Kamel would not have trusted anyone offering them forgiveness and resettlement. But Uday had never been shrewd. A child could see through his schemes. He was not used to having to do brainwork to get his way; his sheer cruelty and reputation would make men cower in his presence. Therefore I would not say I had a lucky escape, as I had never been taken in by Uday's plan. I will always see his approach as just one of his attempts to take control of someone he surely regretted letting escape. Failure might have pushed him to the terrorising measures my family and I were soon to be subjected to.

I decided not to go straight back home to Vienna after the stay in Bangkok, but went instead on a small tour of the Far East to make new contacts in the diamond industry. I visited Tokyo and Shanghai, where I attended a trade fair held annually by the diamond industry. It was a trip which proved to be extremely valuable. My circle of business associates grew and as anyone in business knows, contacts are everything. I also visited Laos and Cambodia, two indescribably beautiful countries which in no way deserved their tragic histories.

Business was going better than I could ever have foreseen. The income I was generating was making me more than wealthy; some months I brought in as much as four million dollars. I bought a building that contained four apartments and had my office on the top floor, while we lived in one of the other apartments. Every so often, however, I was to receive another reminder that regardless of wealth, my family and I were still vulnerable humans made of soft flesh and fragile bone.

Halfway through a hitherto nondescript day, my family and I were leaving our house to go out for lunch in a Viennese restaurant. I had retained the services of several bodyguards, such was the real danger that we would be the target of attacks. One of the guards halted us as we reached the door. "Latif," he ordered, "please don't go to the car. We think someone has been tampering with it." Another of the guards was lying on the road, taking a cautionary look on the underside. He came back towards us and said that the Special Branch would have to be called – he was sure that a bomb had been planted.

Within half an hour the whole area had been closed off, its residents and businesses evacuated. One sharp-minded bodyguard suggested that I run up to my office and fetch my camera, which I did. He was suspicious that the Austrian government would deny that any of this had happened, or that it was just a false alarm. He stayed around and photographed the special police in their every action, culminating in his snapping them removing a bomb from beneath my car.

The bomb had been crudely wired up to detonate when I turned the ignition key. Had the would-be assassins been a little more meticulous, the bomb would have gone off, and that would have meant certain death not just for me but for my family. We owe all our lives to the professionalism and courage of those bodyguards. The event had proved that every penny I spent on their protection was in reality priceless. It took my family several days to recover from the shock, but there was a long-term benefit in the shape of a heightened sense of vigilance and a life-preserving suspicion of everything. I would rather my family had not needed to be brought up in this kind of environment, but they were in it too, now, as none of those plotting against me would go out of their way to spare them if it meant that I could be eliminated. This had been the second attempt on my life since I arrived in Vienna. I was sure that the Iraqi embassy, assisted by the blind eye turned by the Austrian government, was responsible. Were I to be silenced it would save them both a good deal of embarrassment and danger. All they needed was a lucky strike and I would be wiped out. It seemed that every intelligence agency had an angle on me and they all knew perfectly well where I was at any time. I decided on that day to move away from Austria. My presence was a risk not only to myself but to my children and Nusa.

I sold everything I had – many bargains were had by lucky buyers; I did not care about losing money on a deal – it had to go. Property, vehicles and other possessions all went in my desperation to free myself and my family from this city, this country. Every schilling of my money was transferred to banks in London and Switzerland. I knew little of these countries' records, but I was determined that no Austrian financial institution would benefit from my wealth.

An outsider might justifiably wonder why I had stayed in this odious country as long as I had done. Part of it stemmed from the fact that I had, after much pain and misfortune, managed to become a successful business owner, and any move might have resulted in my having to start again from scratch. I also understood German relatively well, and German was a language that was not spoken widely outside of northern and central mainland Europe – any move would require a new language to be learnt, as English and Arabic were the only other ones I knew. There was also the problem of seeking asylum in another country. At least in Austria I did have a passport and was at the time officially recognised as a political refugee. We had also built up a small circle of friends in Vienna, whom we would surely have missed had we uprooted ourselves. Another point, which might at first appear to contradict these pluses, but in fact was an assisting factor, was that I was spending less and less time in Austria – I was travelling the world, mainly on business, and my experiences of Austria came in doses rather than as a constant theme. This might have extended the novelty value of living there, and accentuated the positives or at least lengthened their natural lives.

Most of the minuses, such as the attentions of Kessler and his ilk, had been somewhat moderated since my encounter with the judge, even though I still felt like an outsider and most of the population did little to change my mind. But in the end, Austria was always going to be a temporary home, it was simply that events had forced me to stay a little longer than expected. With the threats to my family's lives, however, a threshold of tolerance had been overstepped, and I was not going to wait around for the next murder attempt.

On reflection, I had been put through anguish beyond my own limits for much of my time in Austria, but cannot look back on my time there as a complete personal catastrophe. When things were going well in Vienna, I was allowed to have a lifestyle beyond anything I could have dreamt of, albeit without any help from Austria itself. I spent many an afternoon in the company of presidents, prime ministers and monarchs, being as I was a successful entrepreneur with a turbulent past. A national day would rarely slip by without my being invited to the embassy of the country concerned for a party or reception of some sort. Some of the world leaders became my friends, and remain friends to this day. We would often exchange favours or give favours on credit, an arrangement which allowed me to get a foothold in many of the world's capital cities, which would stand me in good stead when a new business venture dawned on me.

Horror and advantage confronted me in that country; on balance, however, my fond and dreadful memories of it always tip towards the latter. I can never ignore the fact that without the intervention of a certain judge – or with the success of my suicide attempt – I might have died in that bleak, unforgiving prison cell. That kind of memory can overwhelm the mind somewhat, and mine became a mind that had been made up. We were leaving.

* * * * *

We were not sure where we would end up, but I needed to go somewhere from where I could conduct business and hopefully attain citizenship. An

English-speaking nation would be preferable. On 8 March 1995 my family and I left Vienna behind for a new, and hopefully safer, life in London.

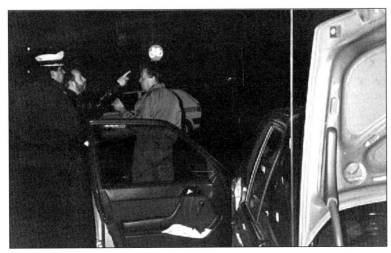

Austrian bomb squad in Vienna searching Latif's car, February 1995

Jorg Haider of the Freedom Party of Austria with Saddam in Baghdad

- Chapter 5 -
United Kingdoms

I had no visa to work in London and my immigration was not authorised, so I thought it best to tell my inquisitors at the airport that we had come to the city for a holiday – and for all I knew, that might have turned out to be the truth. The only official identification I had with me was my Austrian travel documentation, and I was relying on a little leniency, gullibility or indifference on the part of the inspectors. National security back then was a little less tight than it was later to become, but it was still necessary to stick to one's story and avoid doing or saying anything that might arouse suspicion. The chief concern alluded to at customs was that I might be a benefit tourist; this was the time when illegal immigration, asylum seekers and benefit "scroungers" were dominating the moribund Conservative government's agenda, shadowed (or more likely led) by the country's influential right-wing press.

"Do you have any money with you?" asked the immigration official. When I opened up my bag, which contained about £55,000, the official smiled, said "Welcome", stamped my documents and concluded the encounter with the statement that I could stay for "Three months." That sounded long enough for me to get settled and attempt to gain asylum.

Straight away I rented an apartment in the leafy, affluent district of Kensington. My next call was to my solicitor, Mr Silviti, a Lebanese Arab. He would be my vital means of applying for and hopefully gaining asylum in the United Kingdom; this time my refuge was from persecution not from Iraq, but from Austria, and we both thought I had a good case, considering all that had happened to me. I was warned by Mr Silviti that my application could take some time. In the meantime, I had to send all my identification and travel documents to the Home Office. Instead of procrastinating on arrival in this enormous, lively city, I made sure I kept going by setting up a business buying and selling property. This usually involved converting houses into flats and studio apartments and selling them individually – a lucrative operation when done correctly. The business proved successful.

Before long I realised that London, which is a great, cosmopolitan city and a magnet for would-be immigrants from all over the world, was reasonably welcoming and easy to settle in. Compared to Austria, my prevailing sense was of being ignored, which is far preferable to being openly harassed. I soon started to make connections with members of the business community. Practically everyone I dealt with in London spoke glowingly of America. It was a place I had never visited, and before long I got itchy feet and wanted to head west to sample the fabled lifestyle for myself. There was a problem, though – all my travel documents were in the possession of the Home Office. Unless I was specifically invited to the United States, I would not get through their immigration checks and would be put on the next plane back to Heathrow. There was another way, however.

The land of the free welcomed my family and me onto their soil with a customs officer's cursory glance at my forged Dutch passport. It was a good copy and would have survived more intense scrutiny, but I was still relieved when it was not queried, as it was now my only means of getting from place to place around the world.

I had no particular business in mind. It really was a holiday, and my two goals were to experience Hollywood and Las Vegas, those two archetypal American locations famed around the world for excess and chasing the dream that seems to keep the country going. Hollywood proved to be a place of fun and merriment – pretty much as I had expected. Poverty and lavish riches were on display in equal measure; after all, the fabulously wealthy need people to clean their homes, nanny their children, park their cars and serve them in restaurants. My stay in Las Vegas was a sumptuous experience. I swanked between my luxury hotel and the casinos with Babylonian abandon, gambling, eating and drinking as much as my heart would take. I did not care how much money I lost – I was enjoying it all too much. The kids loved Disneyland, but I decided not to go there; they enthused about the place all the way home.

After two weeks' vacation I returned to my London home and resumed my life as though I had never been away. I had not been missed, which pleased me.

It was at this time that Nusa and I had another split of sorts. I received concrete proof that Nusa had indeed been sleeping with another man while I was in the Austrian prison. The "other man" also happened to be William, the photographer who had introduced me to Senta, and who had been (and for all I knew still was) his own girlfriend. It turns out he did not just go for the older woman after all; and that the Austrian prison guards' stories and pictures of Nusa's infidelity had in fact been true – but still devious, nevertheless. Nusa was apologetic, although I doubted her sincerity. Her desire for us to get back together seemed to be real, but I felt a betrayal that I would not easily be able to shake off. The fact that I had at the time been in captivity and utterly powerless made it seem all the more acute. I blamed myself for getting involved too deeply with Nusa in the first place. An institutionalised prostitute like her will not turn into an angel overnight, no matter how much money you give her, I thought. It was true of all the ones I had met in Baghdad, too. Life is not like *Pretty Woman*.

I suppose I did not have strong feelings for Nusa anyway, and the fact that the split was relatively civil proved it; we shared a house but slept in separate beds, this of course for the benefit of our children who had put up with enough heartache in their young lives. I never felt any yearnings to tip-toe into her bedroom at night. As long as our children did not question whether mummy and daddy were an item, we were content, and they were too young to notice any subtleties or even know anything about parental relationships. Another illustration of the civility of our split was that we could agree on keeping a joint bank account. My life could have been cut short at any corner, and without any form of income Nusa would have been dependent on charity – or a return to her old career. Our children would have suffered terribly, and that is something I would not stand for. They were not to blame for my errors of judgement.

Latif Yahia being interviewed by Ed Bradley of CBS "Sixty minutes" 1995

Edgware Road, London, was the scene of the third attempt on my life. It was halfway through the May of 1995. I was walking along the pavement when five men with knives, and speaking Arabic, leapt out from somewhere and started thrusting their weapons at me. I am convinced that they were attempting to kill me rather than scare me, because several of the lunges would have landed had I not managed to evade them. Fortunately for me, the assailants were unprofessional and uncoordinated, and I still had my martial arts training alive in my mind; I made an escape on foot. Again I was lucky to get away with minor injuries. I had no doubts about who was behind the attack. I had not long before done interviews for Channel Four television and the Guardian newspaper, in which the blame for the previous assassination attempts and for my ill treatment in Austria was laid squarely with the Iraqi government. I see this as a grave mistake on my part as I had failed to investigate my own allegations more thoroughly. It turned out that I was blaming the wrong side.

I had been introduced to Ahmed al-Chalabi in 1992 at the conference of Iraqi opposition in Vienna. Although I had a vague knowledge of who he was, he did not strike me as being important or powerful. In 1995 I met King Hussein of Jordan, and we discussed the situation in Iraq. When I spoke about the conference and the self-promotion of al-Chalabi, the king stopped in his tracks and began to tell me something about al-Chalabi's history. He had been the head of a major Jordanian bank, and was found to be embezzling staggering amounts of money from it. He was promptly sacked, but it was too late for the bank itself, which collapsed soon after. Al-Chalabi himself fled to America, where he somehow gained the trust of the administration, who favoured and funded him as a possible successor to Saddam Hussein in an interim administration should the latter be deposed or defeated militarily. There was no reason for me to suppose the king was lying.

The story of the assassination attempt against Latif in London as published in the Guardian 25/05/95

I wrote an article which was published in several Arabic newspapers, damning al-Chalabi and the dishonesty which seemed to be being rewarded across the Atlantic. This was the first time he had been openly criticised; he was being groomed for far greater things, and nobody was prepared to suggest that America's favourite was a criminal. When the Iraqi National Congress was formed, he became the natural choice to be its leader. He was to be unquestioningly believed. The support he was receiving from America was, it was generally accepted, worth ignoring for the prize of US-backed democracy and, perhaps, the overthrow of Saddam. I had made a powerful and politically omnipotent enemy.

Al-Chalabi wasted no time in trying to undermine me. He used his close association with the British intelligence services, MI5 and MI6, to attempt to discredit and silence me. According to him, I was an agent of Saddam and Uday Hussein – how else could I account for my millions of dollars? He said that my open criticism of the regime was merely a smokescreen and that people in the West were apparently unable to penetrate it. My refusal to work with any of the opposition groups was, he reasoned, proof of my true adherence. In his version of events (which I believe he knew to be false), my failure to use my position and my inside knowledge of the regime to foment activity aimed at Saddam's overthrow was merely extra evidence of my support for Saddam.

(In 2004, after Saddam was finally overthrown and discovered in his infamous spider-hole, al-Chalabi's home was raided by the occupying American forces. They suspected him of passing secret information to Iran. Indeed, al-Chalabi is believed to be one of the sources responsible for pro-viding the US with false information about Saddam's invisible weapons of mass destruction, which in turn led the US and their "coalition of the willing" to break from the UN and remove Saddam militarily, claiming a WMD-inspired sense of urgency. However, having his house raided by the US had the effect of endearing al-Chalabi to many Iraqis who were sick of the occupation – he was somehow seen as "one of them", as many Iraqi families had suffered midnight raids by US forces to round up terrorists and criminals. His party had a strong showing as part of the Shia bloc in the January 2005 elections, proving at least that US backing is not always necessary for electoral success in Iraq; although who would ever have heard of al-Chalabi were it not for US funding is debatable.)

As I have described, the truth about al-Chalabi's allegations was very different. I would not be paid to oppose my country. I would oppose the regime holding a noose around my country's neck, but it would be on my own terms and for free. Perhaps people could not understand my reluctance to capitalise on my situation.

Still, it was MI5 who informed me that the May assassination attempt had been the work of al-Chalabi, not the Iraqis.

Both MI5 and MI6 had, like all the world's other intelligence agencies, approached me with offers of employment, but by this time I was used to turning down intelligence work and treated the British with the same courteous knock-back as I gave to all the others. Britain was, in fact, one of the few countries never to have approached me during my time in Vienna. They ended up urging me to open up a business in the United Kingdom, for example a solicitor's or a shop, and they would grant me immigrant status – and a passport – on the understanding that I devoted time to organising an anti-Saddam movement.

None of the intelligence agencies chose to understand my core belief – that overthrowing Saddam would be a good thing only if it did not harm the Iraqi people, which is exactly what their proposed insurgency or a foreign-led invasion would inevitably lead to. I was anti-Saddam, and that was the end of it. (And I was as bored of repeating it as you must be of reading it.) If I could come up with a peaceful means of deposing the regime, I would probably have put it into action by then. I was confronted with a situation that was later typified by George W Bush's notorious post-9/11 statement that nations were either with the coalition (that is, the US), or with the terrorists. There was no way in his view that a person could be opposed both to American military aggression and to terrorism – as though one of them was good and the other bad. People could not see how someone who strongly opposed, *and* had suffered under, the regime could fail to support aggressive action in his homeland.

It was inevitable that my presence in London would before long arouse the inquisitions of the countries that had been directly involved in the Gulf War, and so it did not come as a surprise when both the Saudi Arabian and the Kuwaiti embassies invited me to meet with them – this time officially rather than informally, or as a seditious networking opportunity. Visiting embassies was quite normal; I had visited both countries' embassies in Vienna on several occasions, such as the time I met Kurt Waldheim. The Kuwaiti embassy was particularly anxious to talk to me. I met the ambassador at one of his social events; he was characteristically cordial and respectful to me, congratulating me on my escape and on the work I had done since. I wondered what he was after. It was then that he asked if I could meet him a few days later to discuss some important issues; we made an appointment. I was taken to the ambassador's personal residence, where various Kuwaiti dignitaries – some secretaries, the minister of justice, the foreign minister, the ambassador himself – were gathered. There was also the minister of a newly-created government department that dealt solely with the prisoners and hostages still missing four years after the end of the Gulf War of 1990–91. A perfect meal had been laid on and we ate together.

After the meal we sat down in a comfortable sitting room and I discovered why they had been invited to this meeting – I was asked about the 650 prisoners and hostages, their whereabouts and their wellbeing. They had been assured by members of the Iraqi opposition that they were alive. I knew that they had rewarded the messengers of good news financially.

"So, if you have any information on the prisoners, we would be more than grateful if you could share it with us. The families back home are awfully distressed. If at least we know where they are being held, it could be of enormous benefit to all of us."

"Do you want the truth, or do you want more lies?" I solemnly replied.

"The truth. It has been several years since we had confirmation that they were alive."

"Okay," I sighed. "They are dead. All of them."

One of the ministers leapt from his seat and started to gesticulate, shouting,

"This is not true! We have had assurances!" (The assurances had come from al-Chalabi, al-Talabani and al-Allawi, but they were not to know that their veracity should have been checked.) "We've had letters and all sorts of proof."

"I'm sorry," I said, "but I witnessed many of the murders myself. I can draw you a map. I can tell you how they were killed. I can point you to their graves. The orders came from Uday and Qusay themselves."

The air hung heavy with shock and despair. The gathered dignitaries had no doubt expected that I would be able to give them some news that would at the very least point them in the right direction, give them some hope. Maybe there had been plans to rescue them, or to tell the Americans to avoid bombing the area. But their silent, grave faces spoke volumes. This was not the news they had come to receive, or to take back with them to Kuwait. That was obvious by the light-heartedness on display earlier.

I dipped my head and rubbed my face, then looked up at them. "Look," I began, "if you don't find the graves, then I am a liar. If you do find them, stop supporting these criminals that go under the name of the Iraqi opposition."

I asked for a sheet of paper, and began to draw a map with a road leading out of Baghdad and with a marker showing where one of the mass graves was situated, then proceeded, to their dread, to add more and more locations, with estimates of the numbers of victims at each site.

The Kuwaitis had been paying the opposition substantial sums of money for false information, this I knew. They had not being drawn maps detailing the settings of atrocities; they were causing the hopes of families to be raised and keeping employed a purpose-installed minister on the basis of misinformation from people denying that they lacked the requisite insider knowledge and motivated by their seedy financial gains. I knew I was right, but it would take longer for the truth to sink into the minds of these representatives and the prisoners' friends and families back in Kuwait. How I would have loved to have been proved wrong, to find out that what the opposition had been comforting the Kuwaitis with was in fact true. But my own eyes do not lie to me.

* * * * *

London is a teeming city, with a population of over seven million and an area of over 600 square miles. Every race, religion and nationality is represented within its growing boundaries, and it utterly dominates the south of England culturally, commercially and historically. What is less known is that it is also the capital city of the world's intelligence. Arabic, Israeli and American intelligence services work the streets and the telephones, gathering information and, sometimes unwittingly, sharing it with other agencies. Because of the enormous racial and religious mix in the city, a spy from practically any culture can blend into a given community and start work.

Saudi Arabia is particularly well represented. It is a country where the rights of the individual barely exist – and if you happen to be a woman, a life of servitude (whether voluntary or not) is the height of your ambitions. The ban on alcohol is non-negotiable, and anyone caught in possession of, or trading in, the substance can expect a harsh punishment. Suspicion is often enough evidence for a lengthy spell in prison. The official reason for Saudi Arabia's harsh, prohibitive legal situation is that it is a Muslim state, indeed it was the first Muslim state, and shari'ah law must be the basis on which all other laws are founded. This would be acceptable enough, were it not for the fact that the Saudi royal family and government take advantage of their stays in London to break every ancient Islamic code there is, as though Islam is practised on a jurisdictional basis. Hotels will stock up on champagne when they know a Saudi prince is on his way. Not that staying in a hotel is a necessity – they all have expensive apartments in London's most desirable districts, where they can pamper themselves without care and without fear of being spotted. Nightclubs, wine, prostitutes, casinos and other indulgences that would be unthinkable back home are common among the visiting Arabic ruling classes. To them, the Islam to which they ostensibly adhere is seemingly little more than a convenient way to control their population.

The end of the first Gulf War in the early 1990s, and all the upheaval it caused, was the precursor of a huge exodus of Arabs from Baghdad to London, some to escape harm, others to escape the regime they had become too close to. Many of them started working for the Saudis, as chauffeurs, pimps, spies, and in a variety of other positions. The Saudis also employed other Middle Eastern and north African émigrés, solely to act as eyes and ears in the capital, keeping watch on anyone or any organisation deemed suspicious or dangerous. The right amount of money could buy these Palestinians, Lebanese and Iraqis, and money was an asset the Saudis had effectively unlimited supplies of. If an anti-Saudi publication, news story or broadcast were to be discovered, they would report it to the embassy and action would be taken. If the report was in its preparatory stages, they would pay tempting sums of money to the journalist or newspaper not to run the story, often backed up by the threat of legal action or other more sinister, unspoken threats. Should a book or newspaper make it to print, they would send legions of agents out to buy up every single copy they could find from newsagents and booksellers. The Saudis – and the Kuwaitis – spent many millions of pounds silencing their critics in this way.

The main exiled Saudi opposition parties are also based in London. Opposition is nothing more than a sham in their homeland, so such measures as exiling the dissenters are unavoidable. The opposition consists of educated and intelligent people who can put forward the kinds of questions the Saudi powers can avoid back home owing to a monopoly on all media. (Even the internet in Saudi Arabia must pass through a main filtering server which allows central censorship of information passing both ways. The filter can be circumvented, however, by dialling up a service provider outside the country, which is what most people do, despite the risks. Strangely, countries like North Korea are heavily criticised for such mass censorship, but Saudi Arabia is a special case.) I met al-Misari, one of the most prominent opponents, at a gathering of businesspeople in London. He personified respectability, refinement and intelligence, and I was immediately enthralled by his charm. It was clear why the Saudis would prefer him dead. He was an effective debater, unflappable and reasonable when faced with any challenging questions thrown at him. Should he ever have got the chance to debate face-to-face with the overfed and underchallenged Saudi rulers he would have humiliated them without breaking into a canter. We became instant friends.

It did not take the Saudi-sponsored eyes and ears long to sense my new friendship. I knew this because, in their subtle way, they had started to invite me to the kinds of parties and receptions at which my attendance would hitherto have been deemed inappropriate. I was all of a sudden their most precious friend, supposedly grateful for all the free lunches and fresh connections. That they had ulterior motives was of no surprise to me, but at the time I could not work out what plans they had for me; I was merely following my father's advice to keep my enemies close to me. But just how much I should have considered them my enemies became clear during a June 1995 appointment at the private residence of a Saudi official.

At the reception I was taken into a side room where I met some members of the Saudi Arabian intelligence services. I was asked about my connections with al-Misari which I refused to answer – my private business was nothing to do with them. They tried to assure me that the people I was dealing with were liars and traitors who were opposing the Saudi regime simply to earn wealth and power.

"These people," I replied, "are not after money. Most of them are already rich. Tell me the same things about the Iraqi opposition and yes, I'll agree with you. But these are different."

In a slow, impatient voice, One of the men then asked me, "So do you know Sahid al-Fahri Hamid al-Misari?"

"No," I replied.

The man smirked triumphantly and leant down to reach beside the table. He came back up opening an envelope, the contents of which were spread out on the table in front of me. "This is you with al-Misari," he said. "Why do you tell me you don't know him?" He leant back to await my reaction.

"Look," I stormed, "this is a private matter. I don't have to answer to you.

It's none of your business." They did not push the issue any further, and we all made our way back to the reception. The arrogance on display was stunning. Why should I have told them anything? I was not in Saudi Arabia, I was not a Saudi and I could make friends with whomever I chose.

Latif Yahia with Sharif Ali bin Hussein and Saddek AL-Mussawy in London 1995, these gentlemen took part in the interim government after the fall of Saddam 2003

Ten days later, I was approached again, this time by a member of the royal family. He said he wanted to talk to me. Characteristically, I agreed. At his house in London he greeted me with all the contemptible, wafer-thin sincerity that I had expected, but he soon got down to business.

"Latif," he started, "I know you are a wealthy man, and won't be swayed with petty financial offerings. But we just know that you are mixing with the wrong types, falling for their charms, believing their lies."

What happened next made my heart race. He produced a small canister, smaller than a thimble, then started talking in a pleasant, businesslike way, as though he were ordering food from his favourite restaurant. "I'd like you to invite al-Misari to your house, and you can offer him a drink, some food, anything. Simply pour a tiny amount of this into whatever you give him." The canister obviously contained a concentrated or particularly deadly poison. "And here is your prize." He placed three million pounds on the table, and looked up at me through his dark eyebrows to take in my reaction.

I was in no position to refuse there and then. After what I had just witnessed, that would have assured my death, and since I could not have trusted the British government to pursue the matter, there would be nothing to stop the Saudis from simply rubbing me out of existence. That would not be anything out of the ordinary for this brutal regime. They must have thought that I had nothing to bargain with. After all, I had plenty of enemies for them to blame my murder on. But did they think I would go this far? Did they think they could, at the slightest whiff of three million pounds, change me from being Latif Yahia, well-known opponent of Saddam Hussein, to Latif Yahia, murderer of Saudi opposition campaigners? Murder is not my business. Saudi Arabia is not my country. How could I get out of this situation? Three million ideas ran through my head.

I gave a long, avaricious look at the money. I had to appear tempted. I even allowed myself a shrewd smile; he reacted as I expected.

"Sir," I said after a minute of silence, "your offer is very interesting. And as a businessman, I feel I must at least consider it." I paused again, giving the impression of being torn between my greed and my friendship. I knew only too well how the Saudi authorities treated anyone who opposed them. Like all gangsters they would pay someone enough money to see to it that I was silenced, and go on living their luxurious lives untouched by the law or any pangs of guilt. "Allow me to sleep on it. You will appreciate what a big decision this is." He nodded. "Take your time, my friend. When the job is done, this money is yours. You want an American passport? We'll get you one. British passport? We'll get one. Saudi? Easy. Name your country, we'll make sure you get a passport. Just do this job for us."

"Don't worry," I said, standing to leave, and taking a last, covetous gaze at the money. "I'll tell you my decision tomorrow."

Doors were held open for me as I left. Staff bowed to me. I took a headful of London air, not usually such a good idea, but at this moment it was the air of a kind of escape, a sort of freedom. A kind of air I was beginning to get accustomed to. It was not the same as the sweet air of home. Was Baghdad's breeze as fragrant as I was imagining it? I doubt it. I had almost forgotten. But it was home, the breath of my family, my dear father, whose health or happiness I knew nothing about, but whose presence I felt more sharply than I could have done had he been standing next to me. My father had, through the wisdom he imparted in my formative years, unwittingly saved my life back there in that snake-like tyrant's office. More than ever I desired a return to Baghdad, even if it meant certain death. And once again I found myself stacking a pile of arguments against such a romantic notion.

The moment I sat down in my car I picked up the phone and called al-Misari. "Look," I said, "you are my friend, and I have to tell you something. The Saudis want me to kill you. They have just offered me three million pounds for the privilege. I never have been a murderer and I never want to be a murderer, especially not the murderer of my friend. Not someone like you who wants freedom for his country just as I do for my own."

His gratitude was heartfelt; as he spoke and piled thanks and praise on me , I could sense the gravity of the situation dawning on him, and probably, at last, on myself, too.

The next day, he came to see me. We hugged tightly for several minutes. He kept thanking me for turning down the offer, as though the opposite would have somehow been the normal decision. Maybe he had spent too much time in Saudi Arabia to realise that it was not normal behaviour to offer people money to kill their friends. I would struggle to think of any decent person who would have done it. I tried to accept his thanks graciously but I did not feel like any kind of hero.

"For your safety," I warned, "please don't eat – or drink – anywhere." What the Saudis were cooking for him would not have been on the menu, and it would have been well within their powers to have someone slip a few drops of poison into his order.

Latif Yahia with Abdullah al-Misari (wanted by the Saudi government, he is the Saudi opposition in exile in London. He is currently on the UK's list of deportees)

Every day he phoned me, and I have to say that every day I was overwhelmed with joy and relief to hear his voice. After much reflection, he concluded that the Saudis must have wanted more from me than had been stated in the original offer. Out of 50,000 Iraqi exiles in the UK they chose me, obviously because of my position, not necessarily my closeness to al-Misari. It seems likely that in me they saw the opportunity of an Iraqi opposition figure whom they could bankroll, and they would always have had my guilty secret – that I was a murderer – to fall back on if I stepped out of line. In the meantime I would be a spy, gathering information for them from the echelons of society that were inaccessible to most of their bought exiles, pimps and chauffeurs. Had I wanted to be a spy, would I have spent the best part of a year in a filthy Austrian prison when I could have ended it with a defeated, bloody-faced nod to Kessler? Would I have turned down an American passport and been allowed to live half a world away from the Iraq I had fled? Perhaps every man really does have a price, but mine had not even been approached; and it certainly would not have been in sterling. Could I make it any clearer? I was against Saddam Hussein and his family, not my country. And as for the Saudis, I wanted absolutely nothing to do with them.

Thanks to my book's popularity, my name, and my face, were becoming well known over much of the Arab world as well as in the West. It would not be uncommon for me to be called upon to do a television interview or write a newspaper article. One consequence was that from time to time, somebody would ask me for my autograph. I found this rather funny, as it happens, and I would usually oblige with a chuckle to myself. Because of the reasons for which I had originally published my story – to be given a modicum of security and to protect me from simply "disappearing" – I was not prepared for this kind of attention. Most of the time it was good-natured or curious; other times, I would be subjected to verbal abuse. I used to take my son Omar, then aged about two years, to feed the ducks in Hyde Park. He would love to do this, and there was no such thing as a short trip where Omar and ducks were concerned. Loaves and loaves of bread must have found their way down those avian gullets thanks my little boy. If he was half as happy doing it as I was just spending time with him, he must have been ecstatic.

Tara, Omar and I were on one occasion crouching next to a small pond, trying to distribute our bread evenly between the bullies and the meek among the ducks, when a brown Jaguar limousine purred to a halt behind us. This was nothing too peculiar: the visiting dignitaries would often have a chauffeur-driven "walk" in the park. Saudi princes and princesses in particular would frequent northern cities to escape the searing heat that the oil workers and city dwellers back home could only sweat through. My eye was caught, however, by the people in the Jaguar. And it was not the fact that it was the first stretched Jaguar I had ever seen – even in Uday's infamously well-stocked garage. What did catch my eye was that the driver was female, as were the three bodyguards. They climbed out of the car in a systematic, rehearsed manner, without any attempt at surreptitiousness. Out stepped a fifth woman, obviously the main passenger, dressed in full black burqa, with only a slit for her eyes, but even they were impossible to make out in the shadows.

She strolled towards the pond, towards us, and stopped next to Omar.

"Is he your son?" she asked, stroking his hair. "He is beautiful, isn't he?" Then she turned to me. "You are Latif Yahia," she informed me.

135

"Yes," I said, with a small bow. Shaking hands would have been out of the question – that much I knew.

"I have read your book, Latif. It's very good. I enjoyed it. It's lovely to meet you … wonderful to talk to you." Her voice was beautiful, calm and soft.

"Thank you very much," I replied.

"I'd love you to sign my book for me, but I've left it in the hotel. Would you sign it?"

"Of course," I said. "Next time you are here, bring one with you," I suggested.

"How long will you be here for today?" she asked.

"I don't know. An hour, half an hour." I shrugged and nodded down to Omar. "To be honest, I'll be here as long as the ducks are hungry."

"Could I send one of my girls to pick it up?"

"My pleasure," I said. "No problem." It seems that her girls did not go to the hotel, as they returned several minutes later with three brand new copies, almost certainly from a bookshop in Edgeware Road, just two minutes from the park. The books were Arabic versions.

"Please sign this one with my name," she started … "and this one's for my cousin" … "and this one's for my friend."

I put my little messages on the front pages and handed the books back to her with embarrassed gratitude.

"So what brings you to London?" she at last asked.

"I've moved to London. I run a business. Every day I come here to enjoy

myself with my children and to make sure the ducks are fed."
We spent about half an hour talking like this.

"Will you be here tomorrow?" she asked.

"I'm here every day," I laughed. "Omar loves ducks!"

The next day she was there before me. I parked my little Bentley next to her
Jaguar limousine. She came trotting towards me, or in actual fact towards
Omar, and lifted him up over her head, telling him how beautiful he was.
After the introductions, I could tell by what I could make of her body
language that she was a little uneasy or self-conscious.

"Latif, would you join me for dinner tonight in my hotel room?"

"I'm sorry," I said, "but I don't know you. And I can't even see who you are.
I can't see your face."

"Believe me," she went on, "you must not feel sorry for me. Where I come
from my face is very well known." It was a strange, defensive thing to say; I
had not expressed any pity towards her.

"I can tell from your accent that you are Saudi Arabian," I said.

"You are right," she said. "I will tell you who I am if you promise that you
tell absolutely no one."

"No problem," I replied.

When she told me her identity, I could see why she had imposed this condition: she was a Saudi princess, the fourth wife of a prominent prince who
also held a government position.

"I don't believe you," I said, even though I probably did.

"Well tonight, Latif, when you come to my hotel, I'll show you my passport." She was persistent. I thought she was joking, but she assured me she was not. She gave me another invitation. At 9 p.m. that night I turned up at her suite in the Dorchester Hotel. She dismissed her bodyguards and left herself in this grand, exclusive place with me alone, something I had not been not expecting. She asked me to make myself comfortable and glided into another room.

A short while later she re-emerged, and I was dazzled by what I saw. She was a mirage of desert beauty, her long, flowing hair tumbling over her shoulders, her dusky skin moulded between the contours of her pure face, and those eyes, a lustrous brown but with a damp sparkle that enlivened her every slight movement. Gone completely was the Arabian attire; in its place was a flowing Western dress that cascaded over her shoulders, her hips and her chest. She was twenty-four years old, I soon found out.

I became captivated. My intimate relationship with Nusa was long over, although we remained under the same roof for the sake of the children. She had occasionally tried to rekindle the relationship we had once had, but my feeling that she had betrayed me when I was in prison was overpowering, and besides, our closeness had never in my mind reached any kind of elevated level – even at our best moments it had been a case of mutual support rather than affection.

So here was I, a single man, in a hotel suite with a captivating girl – who happened to be a wife of a Saudi prince. It felt dangerous and exciting. She retrieved a bottle of champagne.

"Where is your Islam now?" I laughed.

"I left it in Saudi Arabia," she said, "it's not here."

I popped open the bottle and we sat down and started to drink and talk. The first glass went down quickly, then the second. By the third glass, we had begun to get a little drunk, and out tongues loosened.

"Tell me, Latif," she said, slurring ever so slightly, "do you love your wife?"

"I'm not married," I replied.
"But you have a son," she gasped her big eyes widening..

"I know, but I'm still not married."

"But that's wrong!" she said.

"What is wrong?"

"To have a child out of marriage! It's wrong!"

"You mean it's against Islam?" I asked. She must have known where the conversation was leading. "You mean it's right that we're drinking champagne now?"

She started to laugh. "You know, this is the system in our head, isn't it? This set of morals." I suppose there is a difference, too. Having children outside of a stable relationship can affect several people; not that all marriages are stable or all cohabitations weak. Drinking alcohol against one's religion, at least in moderation, affects only the drinker.

"Anyway, I'm not married," I muttered quietly, just in case she had forgotten.

"But do you love her?"

"I'm … not … married," I repeated, emphasising every word. "And no, I don't love her. Perhaps if I did I'd have married her by now. But no, I don't. Yes, we live together, but it's for the kids. Certainly not for me." I took a slow sip of champagne. "Anyway, what about you? You're someone's fourth wife, are you not? How would your husband feel if he walked in here now?" She snorted bitterly. "We got married last year and only once has he slept with me. Maybe twice. He may have four wives but even that is not the limit of his sexual affairs. I am nothing more than a small adornment for him, a doll, a trinket to inflate his ego. I see him every now and again. He just walks in, says hello; nothing more." Her voice broke progressively as she talked. Tears began to trickle from her eyes and one splashed onto the back of her hand. "I was forced into this marriage. He threatened my family. He just didn't want anyone else to have me, that's all. This is my life."

I tried to comfort her without crossing any of the makeshift boundaries that I suddenly had to impose on myself. Even though we had shared some closeness, I did not want to take it any further for fear of offending her, although I sensed a feistiness hiding beneath that flawless, obedient exterior. What a waste, I thought, of a woman who seemed faultless but who had been put out to fallow at such a young age, bought and displayed like a carpet that is hung on the wall as decoration.

I went back home that night but felt the stirrings of attachment to this woman. Who would have felt otherwise? She had invited me back the following night.

Our second encounter in her suite became an ecstatic, sensual evening. More champagne was drunk, and any barriers between us faded away and we were sucked into each other's arms. We made love for the whole night.

The clandestine relationship continued for three weeks, with almost every night spent talking, touching and lovemaking. I would have loved to take her out somewhere, to go visiting places and exploring the city, the country, but it was impossible. But even with this stultifying restriction, our time together was heavenly. At the end of three weeks, she told me that she could not live this life any more.

She was going to go to Saudi Arabia and clear things up, then try and move permanently to the UK. She told me she loved me, that she needed someone like me. And I was beginning to feel the same way about her. We had grown intimate way beyond the physical manifestation. She had opened up to me. I knew everything about her – her childhood, her family, her history, her education. Even she did not know why she had chosen me to be the recipient of the secrets she had carried with her. Nevertheless, I could not have her leaving everything she had for me. Although spending my life with her would have been verging on fantasy, I did not feel I could guarantee her anything. I did not even have a nationality.

Three days after she left, she called me. "Latif, I have a million pounds, and I want you to look after it for me until I come back."

"Why are you sending a million pounds to me?" I enquired.

"Please, just look after it until I get back to London."

The money was not transferred electronically – someone simply arrived at my door, knocked, handed me a bag with a million pounds in it and walked away. I had no idea where it was from, whether it had been flown over from Saudi Arabia or despatched from a UK bank. I simply kept it safe in London. Another ten days passed. She arrived back in London. This time she had £500,000 in cash with her. She planned to stay a week. When we met we held ourselves together and kissed like lovers.

"I don't know how to tell you this," she said, looking straight into my eyes. "What?" I mumbled.

"I'm pregnant."

I was shocked. "By … by me?" I ventured.

"Yes. It couldn't possibly be anyone else. My period never came after we spent time together. It can only be yours. I don't know what I'm going to do." There was no way she could have pretended it was her husband's child, and I am not sure if I would have wanted her to.

As far as I was concerned, abortion was not an option. The mere thought of terminating the life of one of my own children made me shudder. "What do you want to do?" I asked.

"I'm going for the last time to Saudi Arabia. I've got millions in dollars, riyals and pounds, and I'm going to bring them back. I'll leave my husband and I want to live here with you." Her eyes narrowed and her voice went hostile and rasping. "Fuck the prince. He can do what he wants. I don't want to live under his thumb any more, and nobody's going to make me. I don't want that life, not now that I've seen what it's like on the outside."

Perhaps, I thought, I am going to end up with this beautiful, delightful woman for the rest of my days. And Tara and Omar will have a little half-sibling to play with. I must admit that although everything had just got a thousand times more complicated, I was excited and was planning for the future with a zeal that injected a renewed enthusiasm to my life. I saw her off at the airport with a lingering embrace. I really did not want her to go, but at the same time wanted her to make her own mind up. She told me that she would be back in four or five days.

The time elapsed, and when she did not show up I started to worry about her. Who knows about her story? I wondered. She was very close to her sister. Perhaps she had told her. She would have known everything. I do not know. What the Saudi authorities were capable of did not fill me with hope. Surely they would not murder her, but they would almost certainly keep her in virtual captivity until her feelings for me wore off. This was the worst I could imagine happening to her.

The exact details will probably remain unknown; but I was later to find out a few of them. All I know is that the Saudi authorities found out about what had happened between her and me. The prince, her husband, ordered that she be tortured to force out of her the reasons behind her decision to flee the country. She was tortured and mutilated until she admitted what had happened. She gave them my name.

Then they cut off her head.

I found all of this out from her sister. I had at last experienced the ruthlessness of the murderous Saudi regime that had until then only been a hovering presence. I was under no illusions about them; they had nonchalantly attempted to turn me into the murderer of my friend. But this shocked me. This was the prince's wife. His beautiful, stolen, neglected wife. They murdered her because of me. They murdered her because she refused to be bound by their oppression, because she threatened to have a mind of her own. Perhaps the thought of her having someone closer to her own age threatened the prince. He would not be able to stand the humiliation, and yet he wielded absolute power over every aspect of her life. Her head was starting to make her body do things he disapproved of, so he had them separated them forever.

This is the Saudi government that I know. It is remote from the appeasing, crawling relationship shared with most of the world's governments, thanks to its oil and its strategic geographical position. The hands that are shaken warmly by foreign secretaries, presidents and prime ministers are soaked in blood. Will people ever see them for what they are? Will the regime's critics ever be treated as anything other than cranks and anti-everything activists? If this all sounds familiar, consider this: Saddam, before he fell out of favour after blithely invading Kuwait, was the darling of the West. He gave women a degree of freedom that existed nowhere else in the region, modernised the country's agriculture and gave great numbers of his people access to the kind of, modern, progressive education that is unheard of in many Gulf nations and won him an award from UNESCO. But the side of Saddam that was known to Western administrations – the brutal, murderous, barbarous, secretive side – was kept from the world's media. Saddam was installed with the help and blessing of the West. They could do this because he was a criminal, and if ever he fell out of favour, his crimes could be brought into the open and his removal would be a formality (so the theory went). Saudi Arabia is at a similar stage of development right now. Opposition is crushed, dissent is punished swiftly and irreversibly. And this is true of the entire Gulf – Bahrain, Oman, Yemen, Kuwait. Be a friend of America and nothing will get mentioned. Support the world's sole superpower, provide it with enough cheap oil to keep its Cadillacs, Boeings and drive-through fast-food joints going, and a blind eye will be turned to your crimes – however heinous.

I was eventually visited by the sister of my murdered lover. She was, not surprisingly, enormously distressed. As the revelations dripped from her mouth they became torrents of tears that gushed from my eyes like I had never experienced before. I had never seen myself as the crying type. I always thought the years of torture and horror had immunised me to human emotions, but I was wrong. I have heard people describe such occasions as the floodgates bursting open, and I cannot put it any better. It was as though something held back for years had finally succumbed to the inevitable effects of pressure and let go without hope of being patched up. It must have been at this moment that I indeed discovered how deeply I had fallen in love with this girl. And now she was gone forever.

Her murderers had also taken with her my unborn child, and therefore a part of me. It was an unforgivable crime and I was powerless to avenge it.

I advised her sister not to return to Saudi Arabia as her safety could not be assured. I told her of the money her sister had left with me, and could see no reason why it should not now pass to her. She needed much persuading. I told her it was not my money, and asked her what else would happen to it. She did have two or three million pounds of her own, so was not in desperate need for it.

The next day I gave her the £1.5 million. "From now on, I am your brother," I told her. "If ever you need anything, just call."

"That is exactly what I wanted you to say," she wept. "I need advice from you. I don't know what to do next."

"My advice to you," I said, "is to leave Britain."

"I could go to America," she enthused.

I laughed involuntarily. "If you go there, you'll just have to put up with the same old shit. Britain and America are friends of Saudi Arabia. They will put you in a box and send you back there, and nobody will know anything about you."

"So where can I go?"

"Go to France, to Canada. Anywhere that isn't a close friend of Saudi Arabia.

Somewhere where there are human rights. But not America ."

The next day, accompanied by my bodyguards, I drove her to Paris via the Channel Tunnel. We stayed there a week during which time I found her a large villa. Saudi women, especially those of the more genteel classes, are simply unequipped educationally or socially to do such things on their own, thanks to the way information on independent living is kept from them by their society. We have seen what happens to women who start to get ideas of their own.

We remained in contact until a few years ago, when our communications ebbed away, taking with them my last point of contact with probably my first real love. Of course, if her sister should call me today I would jump on a plane and go to see her if she needed me. As far as I know she lives in Canada, but could be somewhere else. I like to think that she has found peace, and started a new life. I simply hope she is safe.

And although I have since found a wife whom I love more than I can express, I shall never forget that lost soul whom I also loved and who was bullied, oppressed and murdered by her husband and sections of her government until she met her ultimate fate at the hands of the same unpunished individuals. Nor will I forget the child I never knew, also murdered by the same smiling, egregious bastards.

As far as the Saudis themselves were concerned, they had made for themselves a story which could not only tarnish their refined image abroad and at home, but could also become another straw on the camel's failing back. People would only tolerate so much.

Fortunately for them, the Saudi royal family owns seventy five per cent of the world's Arabic newspapers, and the ones they do not physically own they can exert immense pressure upon to see things their way. More often than not, violence is the dangling last resort; most editors and journalists would accept a large cheque or a bulging envelope instead of running a particularly damaging story.

In my case they saw attack as the best form of defence – that seventy five per cent of the newspapers shouting would drown out any portion of the remainder reduced to whispering as loudly as they could. They started to run disparaging stories about me. According to the reports, I was an agent of Saddam Hussein, and my opposition to him was merely a front. They started to pick holes in my story and made every attempt to discredit me, all no doubt in anticipation of a media assault I was certain to launch, starting with my revelation of their murderous atrocity. Their choice of "sources" was almost embarrassing in its clumsiness. Anyone remotely connected with Uday was considered to have a voice and a story sufficiently valid to add weight to the public denouncement of my character. They dragged to the fore some mechanic or other who had worked in Uday's garage, who looked after his fleet of cars and who had probably never even dared to speak to him, let alone spy on his fiday. Other palace workers, with similar levels of closeness, also banked their fraudulent Saudi cheques. They appeared on television and did newspaper and magazine interviews, all the time spreading lies about me.

I found the whole thing hopelessly unsophisticated and even amusing. I used to laugh out loud when I heard the testament of one of these ridiculous pawns. I vaguely recognised a few of them from way back. It was one of the few links with Iraq that did not make me homesick.

Al-Misari phoned me one day after seeing one such story in a Saudi news-paper: "It looks like the war against you has started now, Latif," he said.

I laughed. "Don't worry," I said. "I know just how to sort it out."

The Saudis must have considered their attempts at softening me up a success, and, like a council of generals preparing to deliver the big push after a lengthy pounding of a distant enemy's positions, they offered me what amounted to a surrender offer. It came in the form of a planned meeting with the son of the prince who had murdered my lover.

He invited me to meet him in Saudi Arabia. This was out of the question. I told him I would meet him on my own territory, which at the time was

London.

We met in the Hyde Park Hilton, in a suite chosen by me, and both my bodyguards and his own checked the room thoroughly before our meeting started. Both entourages entered the suite. I dismissed my bodyguards, and he followed suit.

The meeting started as I predicted it would, with him producing a cheque book.

"Any price you want," he said. "Just say the number."

"Why do you people think that you can buy anything or anyone with your money?"

"I can see you will not take my money," he said. "I just have one thing to ask of you. Please, please, do not tell the story to anybody. I will put a cheque on the table and give you a pen. You can write on it any number you want. Just please do not make this story public." What surprised me more than the sleaziness of the proposition was the fact that he said "please". In all my encounters with Saudi diplomats and royalty, I had never once heard them use this form of cordiality. To them everyone, national subject or foreigner, was a slave, fit only to be ordered about and told what they were to do. It was an astounding demonstration of arrogance but thanks to their money it did not seem to bother those with whom rudeness and lack of respect was part of the arrangement. He continued, "Any photographs you have – and the negatives, of course, you must give them to me as part of the deal."

"I don't want the cheque. I don't want your money. And I'll never forget this woman," I snarled. "She was carrying my child; and your father, the bastard, he cut her head off."

I did have photographs. She had at first left them with me as proof of her identity, but I kept them to look at when we were apart. I also had pictures of the two of us together. Anyone would have been able to see that it was the same person in both images. Any editor of one of Britain's national newspapers would possibly have paid a considerable amount for these photographs. They might not have caused the collapse of the Saudi administration, but they would for sure have screwed the prince in question. He was a very well-known, highly-ranked prince. I have no doubt that the Saudi royal family would have distanced themselves from him and publicly treated him as a outcast, forcing him to admit his wrongs. The royal family could even have benefited from such action; it could have made them look a little less barbarous, a little more caring, as though they were putting their house in order. They were untouchable.

"Listen," I said. "I am not like the Iraqi opposition. I don't accept money from you people so that you can own a part of me and so that I can grow rich. I won't be taking this story to the press, and it's because this woman was carrying my child and because I loved her. This will remain a secret which I shall take to my grave. Just get out of this room, this country, and take your money with you. You cannot buy me."

He took his message back to Saudi Arabia with him. The fact that the prince did not have the courage to face me personally, but sent his son, is all you need to know about these people.Readers might have noticed that I have gone back on my word. I will not be troubled by such a lapse. The Saudi administration, and this prince in particular, seem to have no scruples and I think that now is the time to give to them a tiny fraction of the pain I have carried with me for a decade.

THE WALL STREET JOURNAL 1995

Major kicks out Saddam hitman

By JOHN DEANS
and DAVID WILLIAMS

AN Iraqi hitman operating under diplomatic cover was thrown out of Britain on John Major's orders yesterday.

Khamis Khalaf Al Ajili posed as a junior attache in the Iraqi interest section of the Jordanian embassy as he threatened and attacked dissidents opposed to Saddam Hussein's rule.

But his undercover activities were tracked by MI5 surveillance teams and reported to senior ministers.

Intelligence officers believe he was preparing to carry out assassinations. He is known to have had contacts in both

France and Belgium with Iraqi agents compiling a 'hit list' of anti-Saddam factions.

Al Ajili was also thought to be targeting companies who might be prepared to become involved in sanctions-busting.

The Foreign Office confirmed that he has been given until next Wednesday to quit the country.

'He has been declared persona non grata on the grounds that he has been engaged in activities incompatible with his diplomatic status,' a spokesman said.

Al Ajili is a member of Iraq's Directorate of General

Intelligence, which has masterminded international terrorist activity on behalf of Saddam. He was involved in violent attacks on dissidents in France and Belgium before moving to Britain in August last year.

Britain broke off diplomatic links after Saddam invaded Kuwait in 1990. Iraq's interests are managed by a small team at the Jordanian embassy and Al Ajili was one of three diplomats based there.

Saddam's hitmen have been responsible for a number of assassination attempts around the world, and the lives of leading dissidents who took refuge in Britain have come under threat. The Iraqi National Congress, the umbrella organisation for the main Iraqi

opposition groups, said: 'We welcome the expulsion from the UK of one of Saddam's agents.'

The Congress recently reported that Latif Yahis, who escaped to Britain after working as a double for Saddam's son Uday, had been beaten up in Edgware Road, London.

The expulsion comes with Saddam showing no sign of wanting to improve relations with the West.

Yesterday, Foreign Secretary Malcolm Rifkind accused the dictator of developing anthrax as a germ warfare weapon.

He told MPs: 'This is a clear demonstration of the brutality and irresponsibility of the regime that still rules in Iraq.'

Mr Rifkind said it showed sanctions were still necessary.

Daily Mail UK 26/10/1995

150

- Chapter 6 -
The Darkest Winter

The blow I had received made me ache deeply. The hopes I had built up, the love I had found, had been smashed. A wonderful life had been barbarously ended, and although my sanity dictated that I had to keep asserting to myself that it was their fault, not mine, I could not help but feel a sense of responsibility. The best consolation I could come up with was that our relationship might have been the catalyst for her inevitable murder; and that was no consolation at all. But these are the kinds of fragments of favourable reason with which one tries to comfort oneself after tragedies and atrocities such as I had lived through.

But no amount of reasoning could temper the emotional hurricane that was about to sweep through my being.

I had been away from home on the evening of 3 July 1995. When I awoke I made my way back home. I arrived at 4.30 a.m., and settled down in my bed. Moments later Nusa came into my room.

"Latif, your brother phoned at midnight," she told me.

That would have been 4 a.m. in Iraq; it must have been important. I leapt from my bed, ran to the phone and rang my brother in Baghdad.

I could hear him crying hopelessly, but his words were clear and dignified. "Latif, I know you are strong, and I know you can take anything. But I have to tell you something dreadful. Your father has been killed. It happened today. We have had the secret services round. They told us that we were not to have a funeral or anything."

"Who killed him?" I asked.

"You know who," he said, and the line went dead.

I sat there, immobile, for a few moments, staring at the carpet, and the receiver fell from my powerless hand. No tears came. It must not have sunk in, or maybe I was emotionally empty. I knew how I always thought I would react when my father's death came, but when the sickening news arrived I felt somehow insulated from it. Still no tears. Just silence. I lit a cigarette and took several deep inhalations, staring at the embers at the end and contemplating the wisps of smoke disappearing into nothing.

Nusa took a step inside the room. "What has happened?" she quivered. "My father has been killed," I replied.

She shook her head, helplessly, then said something meaningless like "I'm sorry."

"Just get out of my face now," I told her. I did not need her around at that that moment.

What I did feel an urgent need for was information. How had he been killed? What had happened? Exactly who was it? I was sure that debilitating emotions would kick in soon; I should use this time productively. It was pretty obvious that his murder had something to do with the regime, but was it Uday, Saddam or someone else who had signed my father's death warrant and executed the deed?

I got in touch with a friend in Baghdad. We had a secret code that we used whenever we spoke, designed to make sure we were not tricked by one of the many impostors on the fringes of our lives. "Please," I implored, "could you go to my family's home and bring somebody? I need to talk."

"What has happened?" he asked.

"My father is dead." I made sure I did not say he was killed. I wanted the truth from my family, so wanted to place no preconceptions in his mind.

Two days later I had heard nothing from my friend. Receiving no information made me restless, as it was the very thing I craved more than all else. I did not dare leave my house in case I missed the call, and spent the days killing time, receiving little mental stimulus but with the unending thoughts of grief, anger, and despair whirling around my mind. I went as far as planning the impossible – a return to Baghdad – as it seemed the only way I could find out what had happened. It was ridiculous, of course, but I was desperate. I was sinking so much deeper into despair that I began to lose my own feeling of self-preservation, and did not care if I was killed or tortured – if this was to be the case, it might as well happen in my home country.

On the third day my phone rang, and the voice on the other end was my brother's. The delay had been caused by his travelling to north Iraq, the area under the control of the Americans, where the conversation was unlikely to be listened to by the authorities. He had taken an enormous risk, as my family members were forbidden from leaving Baghdad and were under constant surveillance. He told me what happened.

Late in the evening of 3 July, two of Uday's men arrived at my family's home and told my father that Uday wanted to see him in his office. They said the meeting would not take too long and that they would pick him up and bring him back. The meeting took place in the headquarters of the Iraqi Olympic Committee, the organisation led by Uday more as something for him to do than through any interest he might have had in sport. At 4 a.m. my father was dropped off at home. The family were still awake at home, terrified that he had been kidnapped, tortured or murdered. He said he did not feel well, and just sat there in the lounge, obviously in some distress. In time he started to feel dizzy. Everyone assumed he was tired, as the past few hours would have been a serious drain on his physical resources. But his skin was changing colour, at first unnoticed but eventually unmistakably, to a sickly shade of yellow. He eventually keeled over and took his last breath.

A few hours after he had been dropped off, Uday's bodyguards arrived at the house and imposed the no-funeral rule. They told my family simply to put his body in a grave and unceremoniously bury him. They must have known he would be dead by then, which confirmed to anyone in any doubt that he had been deliberately poisoned. Their rationale was that he was killed because he was the father of Latif Yahia, in their view one of the country's criminals, one of its traitors, who was working alongside the CIA to overthrow Saddam.

In addition to the one in Austria, I had another cousin who was a doctor but this time in Iraq, and he was asked to visit the family home and find out what had killed my father. Soon after, he performed a kind of post-mortem examination, and discovered in my father's stomach some orange juice which contained traces of poison. No doubt it had been offered to my father, whose throat was no doubt dry with trepidation, and he took it without thinking. It is possible that he had been forced to drink the orange juice, but he would have known that is was poisoned and might have attempted to somehow have his life saved during the short time he spent at home. There is no way of knowing.

Once again Uday had shown the depths of his depravity. He had not only murdered my father; he had done so in a way that ensured that his wife and some of his children would be watching in helpless dread as he fatally deteriorated.

There are still those who believe that I was always, and remain, an apologist for the regime that ruled Iraq between 1979 and 2003. To them I am inseparable and undistinguishable from it. I do not owe these people an explanation as to why I despise their beliefs, nor do I seek to give them one; in most cases it would be futile. But if they believe that I would sanction the appalling actions I have just described, they must have no appreciation of what it is to be human, and I care little for their favour.

My hatred of Uday had always been deep, simmering and non-negotiable, but now it was brought to the fore and took on a pathological intensity. It was war. All-out war. I promised myself, vowed in the strongest possible terms, that Uday would not get away with this act. I would not let this slip by unpunished. He had taken the life of thousands, but now that one of them was my father, he had personally engaged a new enemy, and I would go to any lengths to see him avenged. I started planning; my goal was, in no uncertain terms, to kill him. The cost of my father's life would be his own.

Until I had done this I could not rest. And when he was dead, I would go to Iraq and hold a dignified, proper funeral for my father.

I made connections with people I knew in Holland and Belgium who too had been victims of Uday's wrathful whim. I also started to make contacts in Iraq. Since I now had large sums of money at my disposal, I could buy information from any impoverished, downtrodden Iraqi people willing to take the risk; I did not have in mind the moral connotations. My arrangements, and those of my European contacts, soon took the form of a loose organisation. There were plenty of anti-Saddam movements (and pseudo-anti-Saddam movements), but ours was the only anti-Uday movement, formed and functioning with the sole aim of destroying him and him alone, in whatever way we could – physically, emotionally, financially or otherwise. After all, Uday was a possible heir to Saddam's crown, and an Iraq under the rule of this psychotic, evil bastard would be unthinkable.

Information flowed in, and I paid many thousands of dollars for it. Before long I knew everything about his daily life, his comings and goings, his associates, his vehicles, his homes. The picture I built up confirmed to me just how stupid and naïve he was: he had barely changed his routines since I was in his entourage several years earlier! Every Thursday he would visit the al-Mansour district. He would go to the same restaurants, hotels and nightclubs – exactly the same system. It was as though he had a timetable, like a bus company, but it could provide us with a way of getting at him.

My business was one area of life with which I had no complaints, and was probably the only part I felt I had complete control over. Things were going extremely well. I was continuing to buy large houses, convert them into flats and sell them off. This was almost as lucrative as had been the diamond trade, particularly when the buying and selling took place in London, where property prices can reach breathtaking levels. Most aspirational, ambitious graduates and entrepreneurs entering the city could afford a small flat but not a house, so the properties sold well, even though the market dictated that prices themselves were by any reckoning bordering on the exorbitant.

Nevertheless, I ceased to feel any sense of security in Britain. I was being squeezed from all sides – from Saudi Arabia, the British, the Iraqis and, of course, those posing as the Iraqi opposition. The attempt on my life on Edgware Road had indeed been that year, 1995, although because so much had happened since then it was beginning, dangerously, to feel like a distant memory.

My problem was Latif Yahia. He was famous and infamous in equal measure. It was difficult to blend into the crowd, to run my business legitimately and to have a family life of any sort when Latif was around. He was beginning to feel like my own alter ego, my fiday, my bullet-catcher. He was a burden on my children's development and on my own liberty. Here I was, trying to get along in this world which seemed to be shrinking day by day, and Latif would always be there pointing at me, waving his hands around and attracting people's attention.

He needed to disappear.

I began to make moves to leave London and the United Kingdom behind. I started frantically selling everything, just as I had done in my final days in Austria. My money was divided between accounts all over the world, and I sold everything I owned – my cars, my house in Kensington and all my business assets, and stopped buying anything new.

But where could I go to? The world seemed tiny, and everywhere seemed to have some link to Iraq, Saudi Arabia, America, Israel or Britain. Where could I slip in unnoticed and start afresh? Preferably somewhere where there were no people, if such a place existed. That was the only place where Latif would not be recognised.

I continued to blame myself for the death of my father. And I could not see the day when I would forgive myself. I could have stayed in Iraq and faced the music. Perhaps I would have been the one to accept the orange juice, to have my bones broken, my soul forced through the mangle. Perhaps then my father would have been the one blaming himself – for sending me to the same school as Uday, for being wealthy. Who knows? It was pointless thinking about it. All I knew was that he was the biggest thing in my life – my father, my friend, my teacher, my confidante, a line of continuity in a place where arbitrary acts of violence and mayhem kept its inhabitants in fear and obedience. And now he was gone.

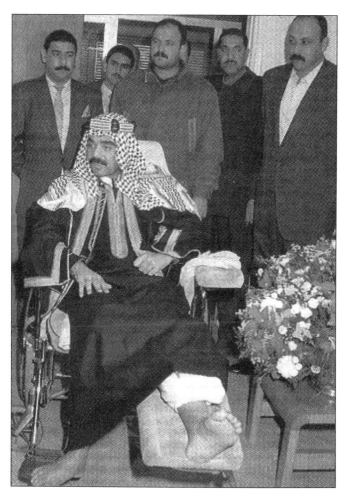

Uday after the assassination attempt in December 1996

One day I realised that I had started talking to myself. I could only assume I had been obliviously doing it for days, maybe weeks, beforehand. It was the first time in my life that I suspected that I might be losing my mind. I tended away from introspection as a rule, perhaps through an arrogance that there could be nothing wrong, but this self-realisation struck me as a warning that I needed to get a grip or lose it completely. My health was suffering, too. This was not helped by the fact that I was a few links away from becoming a chain smoker, which was making me wheeze and cough at the slightest provocation. I was drinking spirits at an alarming rate, and with each glass that was downed I descended into a hazy oblivion that numbed the pain but sharpened the anger. Less than ten years earlier I had been fighting fit – a soldier, trained in martial arts and drilled to a level of lean, efficient, explosiveness and durability that would have been appreciated by an Olympic decathlete. Now I was slowly killing myself from within. I had had psychiatric help in Vienna from Dr.Wolfgang, but after leaving Austria I had not sought any further counselling. Since then I had endured many blows – the assassination attempts and the murders of people dear to me being the most prominent. In retrospect it was inevitable that I would start to feel the pressure of my traumas; but I could not see it at the time.

The loss of full mental capacity went on for months. I had to get a grip of my demons and physically tug them out of myself if I was ever to see my fortieth birthday. The thought that my demise would be being lapped up by Uday – were he ever to be made aware of it – perhaps sparked my resolution not to let my own mind defeat me.

My attachment to Omar was a constant feature throughout this turbulent, agonising period. Wherever I went he was with me, and the balancing happiness that he radiated almost certainly kept me from going over the edge. Tara was equally close, but in Omar I had a blank canvas on which to attempt to form a person with morals, education and courage, all of which would be founded upon the love I had for him. I had been provided with nothing less from my own father, and that part of him would be kept alive throughout his descendants as long as I could influence things.

A letter from Uday to the Iraqi Intelligence services and Iraqi Embassies giving the order to kill Latif Yahia in Norway. This letter was found in the Offices of the Iraqi Intelligence Services after the fall of Baghdad in 2003.

In March 1996 I sold the house in which I had been living, which meant that I would have to find somewhere else to shelter me from the English spring. I checked into a suite in a hotel near Heathrow Airport, not knowing when I would leave.

I would occasionally visit the airport; airports in general held a certain romance for me. I love to travel, particularly when it is not enforced; if I had no commitments I would probably travel constantly, stepping from airport to airport, tasting the flavour of the disparate cultures with each pace. But since I was unable to spend my time travelling, the airport lounge would do for now – I would let the cultures come to me.

I thought I knew enough about central Europe already, much of my experience of the continent being accumulated while being shuttled between temporary accommodations, prison cells and TV studios. I had also seen enough of the Middle East for the time being. But inside me was a wanderlust which had been given a certain injection of urgency due to the events which had been shaping my life and my constitution of late. There was a map of the world in the airport, as you might expect. A country seemed to be shouting its name to me: Canada.

The country is an enormous, sprawling land-mass, with thousands upon thousands of lakes and mountains, and unending expanses of open space and forest to disappear into. There are, of course, the large cities and towns, but if I wanted a completely fresh life, then a rural life – or even an existence in the wilderness – seemed to fit the bill. From what I had heard, Canada's human rights record was reasonably good, and the fact that they had a love–hate relationship with the USA, their powerful neighbour on two fronts, was evidence of a national psyche of stubborn enlightenment, which was attractive to me.

I bought tickets for myself and all the family and without further contemplation of the country or any plans to follow once we arrived, we got on an aeroplane. I watched London fade away behind me and felt an optimistic calmness as we floated over Scotland and then made a long curve to the west for a flight over the sparkling, vessel-dotted North Atlantic.

We descended into what was hoped to become our new, settled life and disembarked, tired and with the potential of jet-lag hanging ahead of us. But thanks to the absence of visas, we were promptly turned around, put back on the plane and sent east across the same ocean and touched down on Heathrow's tarmac within a day of setting off. At least we avoided the jet-lag. We went back to the hotel. As had been the case with my trip to America, nobody noticed we were not there. It was as if we had never so much as passed the hotel lobby as far as the staff there were concerned.

I thought I had gone through all the right channels. I had withdrawn my claim for asylum from the Home Office, and with a little help from my solicitor, had retrieved my passport, which they had been holding. Obtaining a visa proved not to be quite so straightforward. I went to the air-port and watched the destinations rattle across the departures and arrivals board. Oslo – that sounded familiar. I did not have a clue where it was, though.

I went to the ticket desk and asked the assistant, "What country is Olso in?"
"It's in Norway," she replied.

"Oh," I nodded. "Could I have four ticket to Oslo, please?
"Are you sure? You don't seem to know where it is!" She was smiling.

"No, it's okay," I replied, "I'm doing a tour around the world. I want to go to some places I know nothing about. And it looks like I've found one."

"First class?"
"Yes, please."

She laughed and shook her head as she printed out the tickets.

I allowed myself a cursory amount of research on Norway. It looked like Canada in miniature, and is at a similar latitude. I remember wondering whether the language would be hard to master; I imagined not. My previous knowledge of Europe was perhaps a little weighted towards the more powerful and rich countries, the bloc that was run from London, Paris, Rome and Berlin. The fact that I knew little of Norway played immensely positively with me. Perhaps in Norway I could become anonymous again. I could lose myself in its impenetrability.

I did have one link with Norway in the shape of another Iraqi, Abu Taymor, who had left the country in the mid-1970s. He had occasionally acted as a line of communication between me and my publisher. I had never actually met him, but thought I would try to get in touch with him once we were there.

The plane rumbled to a stop on the tarmac, and we set about going through all the normal airport procedures. But I had made another slight misjudgement in my arrangements. Assuming that Norway would be a member of the European Union, I did not bother to attempt to get myself a visa. I was stopped at customs and asked for my identification. I gave them my paperwork and they started leafing through it.

"You have no visa?" I was asked.
"I didn't know I needed it. I am here on holiday," I said.

"Do you have any money?" he enquired.
I was glad he asked this. I had about £16,000 and a wallet full of credit cards.

"And how long do you intend to stay?"
"About a week or two," I told him.

He stamped my passport for a three-month stay.

I booked my family and myself into the SAS Hotel in Oslo city centre, and for six weeks lived from it and did very little else. The change of scenery had done me good, too. I was beginning to feel a little more uplifted. We would have our food in the hotel and spend the days wandering around Oslo. The people there were markedly more friendly than the people of any of the other countries I had blown into.

After this settling-in period, I retrieved my Oslo contact's phone number from my diary and gave him a call. He was affable, warm, and extremely surprised to hear my voice; we arranged a meeting. He visited us in our hotel with his wife, and as we talked it became clear that we had much in common, even down to the fact that we hailed from the same area of Baghdad, Al Azimiyah. We hit it off immediately, although his assertion that my book was brilliant and that he was impressed with my story was slightly embarrassing to take from someone I considered my equal. However, from the start he had a coldness towards Nusa. They seemed far apart, immiscible. I gathered that he had developed a suspicion of her that a non-Iraqi might not have done, I suppose through the subtleties of her personality that would to non-Iraqis have been overwhelmed by the general sensation of foreignness. The attitude towards Nusa was shared by his wife; the two did not seem to pair off as had been the case with other couples we had befriended on our travels. Abu Taymor and I spent the night talking about our lives and our mutual contacts, until the subject drifted to the problem I was experiencing with my identity. "I need to get rid of Latif Yahia," I explained. "He is causing me too much trouble."

"That shouldn't be a problem," he chortled, "this country is full of Iraqis. They seem quite happy to take them as asylum seekers and ask for hardly any form of identification. You just need to think up a name – and remember it. Latif Yahia will cease to exist, except on the bookshelves, I hope."

"So what do I do?" I asked.

"It's easy. Just go to the police station, give them a false name – and don't say you're rich. In fact, say you don't have much money at all. And if they ask how you arrived here, just tell them you came in a trailer or something, you were smuggled and you don't know which route you took. Make up a story to fall back on, too. Make out that you were a soldier or something, and that you deserted. Then say that you want asylum. They'll do the rest."

"It's that easy?"
"Yes!"

"So how do I go about it?"

"Don't worry about a thing. The day you decide to claim asylum, get in touch with me and I'll make sure you don't do anything stupid."

"Okay," I said. "Tomorrow?"

"Tomorrow it is."

The next day he turned up in his modest Datsun and I greeted him into the hotel. He looked me up and down, shaking his head disapprovingly. "Latif, Latif," he said. "We are going to have to buy you some shit clothes. You can't claim to have spent the last three months in the false fuel tank of a lorry wearing a designer suit, now, can you?" We both laughed uproariously. He was absolutely right. My wealth had got my entrance to the country rubber stamped, but if I wanted to stay here as an asylum seeker, it would take a little more guile. There were certain aspects of my life which would need to remain a secret.

"And when we get there, I'll say I found you wandering the streets and that you've only just arrived here. I'll say I speak Arabic and that I have decided to assist you as your interpreter. You can leave all your baggage at my house." We went clothes shopping in Oslo's most down at heel stores, rejecting anything that had even the faintest trace of style, until at last I was dressed like the world's most desperate refugee who had crossed mountains and swam rivers to get to Oslo.

On arrival at the police station I received a shock: the staff were such nice people. In their words, their expressions and their actions they showed more sympathy, compassion and duty than I had seen since I left Iraq. They were sensitive to the plight of asylum seekers and made me feel absolutely secure and welcome. And these were not even asylum specialists – they were merely working on the desk of a police station. My optimism increased.

"Don't worry," one of the policeman concluded, "we'll look after you from now on. You'll be able to treat our country as your own."

They left Abu Taymor and I alone while they went into a back room. My friend turned to me and smiled. "See?" he whispered, "I told you everything would be okay. This country is full of very friendly people. It's not like the rest of Europe." The name I gave them was Iasar. I do not know quite where it was conjured up from. Nusa, Omar and Tara took on new identities and with a bit of luck the old ones would simply fade away – until we needed them again.

"Do you have any money?" I was asked.

I recalled Abu Taymor's advice and said no. They gave me a voucher which would entitle me to a taxi ride to a Red Cross centre in the city, the place where all refugees were initially housed and processed. Everything seemed organised and it felt as though the motivation behind this attitude was no less than the wellbeing of asylum seekers, rather that expedience and cost-saving.

Abu Taymor stepped in and said that the voucher was not necessary, that he would take us there. The police officers looked at each other, then turned back to us with beaming faces and shook his hand, thanking him profusely. "You are good citizen," one said, "helping those less fortunate than yourself." Was there no limit to these people's humanity? I would reserve judgement until I reached the Red Cross.

Once again I was surprised. The room was large, clean, comfortable and airy, with four beds and big windows – nothing like the camps in the rest of Europe which had more in common with prisons. It would appear that nations have laws about prison standards, but that asylum centres slip under the radar and therefore have no such protection. I have stayed in hotels worse than the Norwegian Red Cross centre – and paid for the privilege. We were given access to a doctor, an arrangement which was utterly devoid of any of the sinister undertones that had accompanied the meetings I had had with medical practitioners in Austria. Again, it felt like it really was for our benefit. The doctor's discovery of the injuries on my body from my various misfortunes might even have helped my cause.

The people in reception treated us with more respect than we could ever have hoped for. Concern, reassurance and professionalism gushed from them effortlessly. At no point did I feel like this attitude had been drilled into them. There seemed to be something in the Norwegian nature that endears them to all but Eurovision Song Contest judges – and what do they know?

I gave the story we had agreed upon earlier – that I was a soldier fleeing Saddam Hussein's rule, and that I would like asylum in Norway. They sympathised and granted me asylum almost without question.

I of course wish to take nothing away from Abu Taymor, who treated me with kindness and dignity and gave me the benefit of his wisdom on many occasions. I can say with confidence that in Norway he found his spiritual home. "I'll visit you twice a day," he told me. "I'll bring you food, clothes and whatever else you might want."

The centre housed refugees of many nations, but mainly of Somalia and Iraq. I hardly spoke to the Iraqis since the majority of them were Kurdish. The exception was the two Baghdadis we met there, and our whole family became good friends with them. They adored Omar and Tara almost as much as I do. One of our friends, Hamed, was no older than twenty years old and often gave in to his emotions; tears were never far from his cheeks. By any measure he must have been traumatised. We all did our best to comfort him and make him smile, but I knew exactly what he was experiencing. Out of the blue one day he said to me, "You know, Iasar, I hope you don't mind if I say this, but you look so much like Uday Saddam Hussein. It's uncanny. Did you ever hear about that guy who was his double?" I stood there shaking my head slowly as he related my story. "Yes, I read about it in the paper. He was taken from the front in the Iran–Iraq war …" All I could do was act ignorant and resist the urge to correct him now and again when he veered from the story a little. It would appear that my resemblance to Uday had been the cause of his discomfort. The same had happened when we arrived at Traiskirchen.

After a three-week stay a dwelling became available, in a town at the far north of Norway. It was a town called Boda, about an hour and a half away from Oslo by plane. Abu Taymor assured me that my stay there would probably not exceed a month or two while I was sorted out. We were not the only asylum seekers entering the country.

We certainly hoped it would be a short stay – we left all our possessions, right down to our travel documents, with Abu Taymor in Oslo. Boda was the epitome of my aspirations, lying precisely in the middle of nowhere. The town is little more than a hamlet, being the location of just a small gathering of houses. The landscape was snow-covered and every building had icicles hanging from every water run-off. Two weeks after arriving there, a knock on the door came. I answered and was given a letter: "POLITICAL ASYLUM GRANTED" was the phrase that endowed the letter with as much beauty and drama as I could bear. The letter's contents created a new list of things to which I had instantly become officially entitled. The most important to me was that I could work.

Before long I had bought myself a house, somehow finding one even further north than Boda, which suddenly resembled a noisy metropolis in comparison. It was a barren yet striking place well within the Arctic Circle, and it would suit me just fine until my passport arrived. It was on the border with Finland, in an icy, dark, blue-tinged territory where one's breath turned to steam at the slightest exhalation, and where the sun remained hidden for months throughout the depths of winter. I would struggle to find any parallel with Baghdad.

My house was large and comfortable, with views that could warm the heart. The village was small, and apart from a single Lebanese man, our faces were the only dark ones in the whole region. As for Arabic speakers, I would say they equalled the number of Norwegian speakers in the average Iraqi village.

My next major purchase was a medium-sized boat I stumbled upon. Every day without fail, I would take Omar onto the icy seas and we would spend the days there gently rocking to the rhythm of the waves and doing a spot of fishing. I also took the opportunity to revive my love of painting. The solitude and the peace would have been the envy of anyone who has ever tried to perform this contemplative art in a noisy city.

This lifestyle freaked Nusa out. It was far removed from the life she had made herself accustomed to, the life of luxury and civilisation, where she could go shopping and eat in restaurants and live the materialistic life. Were it not for the children I would gladly have paid for her air ticket to any city in the world. But I for one was going nowhere.

Another dark day, Omar and I went out as usual to fish in the sea, and we noticed an enormous boat approaching us. As it got closer I recognised the Russian flag flapping on a pole. The boat started to slow down and navigate its way towards ours, much to our astonishment. A man started to shout at us from over the side, then he clambered down and introduced himself in English. We had not been talking long before he let me know that he was trying to sell his boat, more in the hope that I knew a potential buyer than in the expectation that that person would be me.

"I'll buy it," I said, barely hesitating.
"No. You're joking," he laughed, but noticed the expression on my face. "Aren't you?"

"No, I'm not joking," I smiled, "I'd love to own your boat."
"Six million krone" he said. This was the equivalent of £600,000.

The boat was a fishing ship, a trawler. I cast my eyes along the hull and took in the state of the vessel in general. It looked fairly sturdy but needed a bit of work on it; to be honest, it looked as though it had been somewhat neglected. I figured that it would cost another £200,000 to renovate it to a state of repair and seaworthiness with which I would feel comfortable. "That's fine," I said. "Six million krone."

"The price includes the staff," he went on. "There are twenty-eight of them." I had not thought about this part. "What are their wages?" "Two hundred dollars a months," he said. This would have been a reasonable wage in their homeland, Russia.
So it was that a new venture occupied me. I bought the boat, had it renovated and with my crew sailed out into the northern seas to trawl for fish, staying out there for four or five days. It was the perfect opportunity to discover that I did not have sea legs – I was unstoppably seasick on these waves, even though it was something that had not afflicted me in my smaller vessel. I went from being the only person with dark skin to being the only one with green skin, but I somehow got used to it by using a few averting

techniques advised to me by my highly amused shipmates. Nevertheless, after we arrived on terra firma, I told them I would not be travelling with them any more. They were welcome to their waves. Instead I would remain ashore and use my business legs to negotiate prices for the trawler's catches and sell the fish to the various companies who produce tinned sardines and such like. This went on for several months.

*   *   *   *   *

Our family were quite settled by the time I received a knock on my door at home from Norwegian intelligence.

"We need to speak," they informed me, stepping into my house.
"Okay," I said.

"When you arrived in this country," one of the agents said, "we gave you respect – you and your family. We granted you asylum within our borders."
"Yes? What's wrong now?" I wondered out loud, Inside, I knew what was coming next.

"What we want to know is why you did not tell us who you really are. The identities you and your families gave us are false." An agent then produced some photographs of me and my book. "This is you. You are not called Iasar, are you? You are Latif Yahia." I nodded solemnly. "You are right. That's me," I said. "But what could I do? I have to look after the security of myself and my family. I needed anonymity. Everywhere I have gone so far there has been an assassination attempt."

One of the agents nodded in understanding, and I did not sense any insincerity. "It's all right. You can stay here. I fully appreciate your motivation. But we will have to tear up the asylum you and your family have been granted and open up a set of new claims. This time they will be in your real names. We will make a new decision on that and get back to you. I can see no reason why you won't be granted asylum in your true persona. In fact, you'll probably have a better chance of being granted."

"Does this mean I am an asylum seeker again?"

"I'm sorry. But we can't give you asylum under a false name. It just can't be done."

"So I have to go through the whole procedure again?"

"Yes," he said, "but don't worry about it. We have every intention of respecting your decision to give false names, particularly in view of the attempts on your life. I'm sure many would do the same. We know that you did it for security, not because you were attempting to defraud us or to mask criminal activities." "No problem," I sighed. But it was hardly an insignificant development for me. I thought I had at last left Latif behind and set out on a new life, but something had stepped in to prevent things from being just as I had wanted.

I had no idea how they had got the information on my true identity. Perhaps they were very thorough; maybe they had been tipped off. After a month of not hearing anything from the authorities, I employed a solicitor to chase up my case. "Of course you'll get asylum," he assured me. "If you don't get it, who will? Yours is a crystal clear case of political asylum. Look at some of the people they let into the country, people claiming asylum when they are in no danger."

It gave me some hope. I had to report to an asylum centre, which had been set up to help refugees rather than to imprison them. It was peopled mainly by Shia refugees from southern Iraq, who had fled south into Saudi territory after the first Gulf War, only to be refused entry by the authorities. These people could not have been sent back to persecution by the kingdom – what would the world say? – so had been kept in a sprawling refugee camp in the Saudi desert until more permanent placements could be located for them. By coincidence one of them was within driving distance of my home, just outside the town centre, and it was to here that I would report.

I got on well with the manager of the camp. We would share jokes and he respected me, although he did not know my true identity. He would pull a chair up in his office when I came around and we would spend some time together, indulging in small-talk. I rarely spoke to the Iraqi inmates, as it would not have been long before one of them worked out who I was.

The night was ceaseless. In the Arctic circle, because of the way the earth leans on its axis as it orbits, the sun never shines in winter and never sets in summer. In spring and autumn it pokes its face above the horizon around noon, but the general feeling then is that of a lengthy dusk, with periods of night-time between. It can alter the body clock and lead to a pervading ennui or depression. And it made Baghdad feel like another planet.

As happened at irregular intervals, I would develop a pining for home. The sensation would often be superseded by the quashing reality after several moments. Going back to the country in its present state, until there was a sign on the door saying "under new management", I was fated to skirt tropic and tundra, city and wilderness, running away from its curse. But were it not for the intensity of the homesickness I was suffering, the travelling would have been a much more mind-expanding opportunity. I had had dreadful experiences in Iraq. They were the very incidents that launched me into flight. But I would so dearly have loved to turn up in my district and greet my family with a hug and a kiss, tell them what I had been up to, find out what they had been doing. Family. Without my father the word had a hollow feel to it. But now, as in the immediate aftermath of my father's murder, was the time we all needed each other. I still had my goals: my vow to give my father the funeral befitting a loved and respected family elder; my burning desire to put a stop to Uday's reign however the opportunity presented itself. But in amongst all that was my desire to go back and live a normal life. With every day it seemed less likely, but without a dream such as this, how else could I go on?

*   *   *   *   *

It must have been four or five in the morning, although it is hard to say. My door received a knock.

"Who's there?" I asked without opening it up.

"Politiet," came the response. (This is Norwegian for police.)

I opened the door. A freezing draught blew into the doorway and I, wearing just my pyjamas, shivered at the silhouettes. There came a lunging motion towards me from one of the visitors. I felt a sharp pain in my stomach. At first I thought I had been punched, and held myself tightly as the two men turned into footprints in the snow as they disappeared into the darkness. A warmth started to spread between my fingers; I recognised it straight away as blood. I had been stabbed.

I grabbed at the phone and called an ambulance, before attempting to stem the bleeding as best as I could. I was taken to hospital and given fifteen stitches and a police guard. I was questioned by several note-scribbling police. Did I have any idea about who could have been responsible? I had learned my lesson from the al-Chalabi episode, and did not jump to the conclusion that Saddam or Uday had sheathed the knife. Nor did I place any suspicion on Saudi Arabia, whose royal family would no doubt have preferred me right now to be freezing to death in my own bloody doorway. I simply could not put my finger on a suspect given any of the signals I had received of late. Blaming the usual suspects is a great way for the genuine culprits to get themselves off the hook; every criminal would love there to be a ready-made scapegoat on whom to pin his crimes. I just shook my head.

My stay in hospital lasted three days, after which I signed myself out against medical advice. Hospitals are, in my eyes, horrible places to spend one's days and nights. I would heal quicker at home.

* * * * *

Nusa continued to be a thorn in my side, and I often struggled to get to the bottom of what motivated some of her actions. Her latest instalment of the infliction of misery she was serialising in my life came when I caught her on the telephone, contacting the Iraqi embassy in Bonn. I found out that she had also contacted the embassy in Vienna. She seemed bent on causing me damage. It was worrying. As the mother of my child, I had given her access to my bank accounts so that should Iraq's tentacles ever make contact with me and eliminate me, at least my children would not go without.

"You bitch!" I screamed. "Why do you want them to kill me? Why do you want to orphan your children? I never thought you would sink to this." In my rage I repeated the threat to her that had landed me in an Austrian prison cell – that I could kill her right now and bury her and no one would miss her. "Why? Why do you do it?"

"I'm sorry," she moaned. "But I was forced to do it. They told me they would kill my sister and my father if I didn't give them information about you."

My body was rigid with anger. "You are a bitch," I said. "I knew a whore could never become straight. Can't you leave me alone or just get out of my life?"

Two days later, I was driving into the town when my car ran out of fuel. I walked to the petrol station and filled up a canister. Being close to the refugee camp, I decided to pop in and see my friend in the office.

"Hi there," I said as I entered.

Nothing. He looked up from his paperwork, then looked back down and carried on writing.

"Hey," I said, "what's up? Why aren't you speaking to me?"

"Because you are a murderer, a liar, a criminal," he seethed. "You were working with Saddam Hussein, and I don't want you in my office ever again! Get out!"

It was at this point that I discovered another trait of the Norwegian psyche, which could go some way towards explaining their apparent affability: they were rather naïve and gullible, especially where politics were concerned.

They had a tendency to believe whatever they were last told. Perhaps it was only those in authority who had this attitude. For sure, it was not always an unattractive trait – indeed, it had helped me into the country in the first place – but its downside was that it could lead to a somewhat unscientific approach to evidence gathering. I am reminded of Alfred Nobel, after whom the Peace Prize, was named. He invented dynamite, and declared that it would end all war, as man would never go to war knowing that he would face an army equipped with this, the original weapon of mass destruction. He had failed to include in his logic the fact that no man would ever go to war were he not sent there by his leaders, regardless of whether he would be facing swords, spears, cannonballs or mustard gas. Nobel's was a pleasant, optimistic sentiment, nevertheless. And the Norwegians have rewarded his good intentions by hosting the Peace Prize since 1901, even though Nobel himself was Swedish.

It turned out that the Shia inmates of the refugee centre had been spreading rumours that I was a member of the Iraqi inner circle, and that one of them had told the manager. Without question, without reason and without hearing my side of the allegations, he believed them over me. He went through his reasons for blanking me out calmly and unemotionally, but evidently hiding a deep mistrust and hatred.

"No!" I yelled. "None of that is true. You don't understand Iraq one bit. The Shi'ites, they hate us. They hate the Sunnis, they hate the middle classes of Baghdad in particular. I was never a member of Saddam's inner circle. How do you think I ended up here? I escaped Uday because he would have killed me! Did you know he killed my father earlier this year? All these people here, they don't even call themselves Iraqi. They hate Iraq. They say they had Iraq forced upon them. They are full of resentment and never miss an opportunity to try and destroy anyone who they see as their enemy, which to them is practically everyone. If anything they call themselves Iranians. These are the messengers who have been telling you lies about me." Then the other side of Latif re-emerged. I was not satisfied with having put my side of the argument forward. Boiling with rage, I started randomly splashing petrol out of the canister and all over his office walls and furniture. I was actually seconds away from getting out my lighter and burning the place down. It might on the face of it seem like a trivial thing, someone not speaking to me like this, but it was everything in the background of the story that was fuelling my rage. I had worked out that someone from the camp had probably been the shadowy figure who stabbed me then fled, and it now felt like the camp itself was out to kill me. And this manager in this office had been listening to the gossip and accusations which were spreading like wildfire throughout the camp. At a deeply subconscious level, perhaps, there would have been some poetry in my creating the spark which would go on to turn this place into wildfire and put an end to the lies and rumours.

I was apprehended by the in-house police officers and they promptly arrested me and threw me into a cell. I am now a firm believer in poetic justice. My stay was longer than I expected: twenty-three days. I suppose my crime had been quite severe, and looking back I consider myself lucky that I was stopped when I was. The prison was not an altogether unpleasant experience. It was comfortable and warm. Just like the Red Cross centre, it had more in common with a hotel than with a prison. I had my own room with a bed and a television, and I was not restricted to my cell. Nusa and the children visited me twice, and while they were here Nusa repeatedly asked how long I thought I would be in prison for. I could not say. I did not feel as though she was anxious to have me back, however.

The guard was as friendly and respectful as most of his compatriots, and provided me with anything I wanted. I never asked for a can of petrol, but cannot help feeling they would have rustled one up. The prison staff did offer to give me satellite television (which would have meant having a dish specially installed) because the only television available was in Norwegian, a language which was mystifying to me. Bail was set, and I took it at the first opportunity.

After checking out, I went home to find that my beloved Nusa had disappeared with Omar and Tara. It did not take me long to discover that she had also taken it upon herself to empty my bank accounts. Wherever she was, she had everything I owned and loved, and I was left with an empty house. It felt like a practical joke. But Nusa was not the joking kind – she really had done it. And something told me she intended it to be permanent, not some little jaunt while I was away or a warning for me to start behaving myself. I now had an explanation for her uncharacteristic eagerness for information on my release date.

I do not know what she expected from her life outside Iraq, but whatever it was I was not providing it and she had made no effort to provide it for herself. I could be convinced that she felt threatened by my outburst, even though she must have known that despite my words I would never have harmed her. I prefer to believe that she was devoid of morals and grabbed at whatever she could get from me. She had the perfect opportunity to start afresh and took it. I wanted her out of my life, but stayed with her for the children. Now she had shown who was number one in her eyes – herself – and in the process had stirred up so much hatred in me that I found myself wishing I had indeed carried out my threats. Prison here was not as bad as what she had put me through. She had not only left me powerless and practically broke, but she had also no doubt left Iraqi intelligence with information about our whereabouts, then left me to their mercy.

The Lebanese man we had befriended could give me no further assistance in locating her, although it did seem that she had visited him to say goodbye.

My love for Omar would give me no peace. In the days and weeks that followed I missed him and spent days and nights crying unstoppably. It was not that I felt he was in any danger – I trusted Nusa at least to look after her own son – it was the sheer heartache of not having him near me, not being able to give him a hug and make him laugh. It was a feeling accentuated by the fact that there was little chance of locating Nusa, sly as she was. She would probably disappear into a city or even go back to the Middle East where she could disappear forever. I simply had no idea what to do next. One thing was sure – I could not inform the police or any other authority, as my own location would get into the system, ready to be picked up by any of the growing number of people who would like to track me down and pay me one of their unsolicited visits. And I could be quite sure that she would not make it easy to be tracked down herself. This spiral of hopelessness simply led to more tears.

There were a few things that Nusa could not get her hands on, however, and I liquidated them straight away. My house and my trawler, and the odd bits and pieces that she could not, or decided not to, take with her all went onto the market and were sold at less than their value, just for quick sales. This got me back on my feet.

But they were homeless feet, eager to move on

Another country beckoned.

- Chapter 7 -
Into the Wasps' Nest

I was not permitted to Leave Norway. This was one of my bail conditions. But there was nothing for me here now, except perhaps a criminal record. Norway had been good to me and I will always be grateful to them for their hospitality and respect, but I felt that it would not be long before I was caught up with, and I did not have much trust in the Norwegians' ability to keep certain people away from me – not that I expected them to.

I got on the train bound for Oslo, and settled down for a journey of twenty-seven hours' duration. However, halfway along the journey, at a station near the Swedish border, I got a sudden urge to alight, and the moment the train squealed itself to a stop I stepped onto the platform with my suitcase full of cash – the half million or so pounds I had raised from selling everything – and a few clothes. It was about four in the morning, but it did not seem to make any difference as I was still in the region of near-perpetual winter darkness. I have to admit to feeling a little uneasy wandering around with all I owned in a suitcase. To anyone who could have successfully wrenched it from my grip, it would have provided quite a pleasant surprise, not to mention a comfortable retirement.

After locating the taxi rank, I approached a waiting car and put my head through the window. "How much would you want to take me to Sweden?" I asked. "I don't care where, I don't care if it's just a village, as long as it's inside Swedish territory."

The driver stopped reading his newspaper and stared at the road ahead. He was thinking. "I'll take five thousand krone," he suggested. This was the equivalent of about £500.

"No problem," I said, "I'll give it to you. Just drive me out of this country."

It was a memorable and occasionally terrifying journey. My driver kindly decided to treat me to a scenic route, although I'm pretty sure there was no other. We forced our way through blizzards, swerved around enormous, humped snow drifts that were encountered with no warning at all, and slid along mountain passes with a sheer drop on one side and which would have meant certain death should the driver lose his concentration for a moment and misjudge a corner. Never have I experienced scenery, weather or blind-faith driving like this before. Of course, I lived to tell the tale, and can only assume that the driver did too after making his treacherous way back home.

Before he left me, however, he told me that I was now in Sweden and that the building opposite was a hotel. He gave the impression that he was an accomplished people smuggler, although why anyone but me would want to escape from Norway is beyond my comprehension. The authorities in Norway would probably give you a map if you told them your intentions politely enough. He also pointed out a bus stop, and said that a bus would arrive which would take me to the railway station where I could pick up a train to Stockholm, the capital city. I paid him and off he went, his engine sounding numb against the snow and freezing air. I was left alone in this tiny village; the sun looked like it was still a few hours away from making its shallow appearance in the sky.

I trudged my way to the hotel and walked inside, blowing the warmth from my lungs into my cupped, blue hands. There was nobody on the desk, so I rang the bell. Nobody came. I shouted "hello?", then repeated it much louder. There came no reply. I soon realised that there was not a single sign of life in the dark building. Just to make sure, I wandered around it, knocking on doors, all the time shouting "hello, hello" and stopping in anticipation of a response. But there was none.

One of the doors I tried was open. I stepped inside and saw a small room with a television set, which I promptly switched on, just to see a human face and possibly generate a little heat. Perhaps the sound of the television would alert someone to my presence. I noticed the coffee machine and, feeling bizarrely like a bearded Goldilocks, helped myself to a cup, just to warm myself up. Was I the only person in the whole village? I could hear nothing but the sub-zero breeze occasionally disturbing something outside. It was a surreal experience, and as I sat down with my icy fingers gripping the warm cup and the steam wafting past my nose, I started to giggle to myself, probably my first laugh in weeks.

It was a happiness that was soon frozen out of me, however. There I was in this tiny, frosty place with no friends, no family, and no Omar. Most of the money I had built up was gone, probably as we speak being spent or hidden away by Nusa. The situation focused my mind on all that was wrong, and it was difficult to see how things could get any better – or worse, I supposed, optimistically.

The past must have been dormant in those dried Arabica coffee beans; the inhalations and the taste started to enliven that part of my brain devoted to all that I missed about Iraq – my mother, my sister, Baghdad itself. And I could not leave my father out of the list of people I longed to see. The image of his face, and the sound of his voice, melted into my soul and the now-familiar tears were not far behind. Each time I cried felt a little different, had a different spark and came in a unique manifestation. This time my tears were the maddening, helpless sort. How I longed for a glimpse of the sun, for the snow to turn to sand, my shivers to sweat.

If I wanted ever to see my beautiful family again, I would need to face the reality – that it could be years before we met again, and that if I did not keep a close watch on my sanity our meeting might not even take place. I needed to remain alert, inquisitive and enterprising. But nothing would take away the pain and longing, and I would have to work hard to prevent the demons from guiding me away from my determined path.

There were also more practical difficulties to overcome, such as not having a passport or any kind of identification. The documents I did have were in the hands of the Norwegian authorities. The implications of smuggling half a million pounds across the border were unknown to me; I will probably need to keep quiet about that for the time being, I thought.

The village did eventually, scarcely, stir. I heard the occasional car engine, about one every half hour, but apart from this the place seemed to be in a state of partial hibernation. I could not think where these people were coming from or going to, as there seemed to be no sort of industry or entertainment to be had. Perhaps I had died and was in the reception area of a kind of frozen hell, the occasional visitors passing through on their way to their ultimate destiny. When a more substantial diesel engine made itself heard, I knew it must be the long-awaited bus and, grabbing for my suitcase I bolted out of the front door of the ghostly hotel; this was one bus I could not afford to miss.

I ran as swiftly as I could through the unforgiving snow, across a small square, occasionally landing on some unexpected object beneath the surface. I tried to call the driver not to go away, but was panting, partly because I had exploded to life from being seated for a few hours, partly because I had let my fitness disappear. My lungs burnt. I had images of my suitcase flying open and £600,000 fluttering around the village. But I was determined not to miss this bus, and pushed myself through my self-imposed pain barrier until I could once again hear the rumble of the engine over the throbbing of pumping blood in my ears and the rasping gasps emitting from my mouth. Through the puffs of vapour billowing out of my mouth, and bent double with my hands resting on the side of the bus, I thanked the driver for waiting and asked if he was going to the Stockholm-linking station, trying my best to explain that I was not from round here, and understood no Swedish. He calmly informed me that he would not be leaving for another hour and a half, so I should make myself comfortable. The driver must have watched my desperate dash towards him with amusement, but not the hateful kind. He was welcoming and friendly, even though he had no particular need to be, rather like most of the Norwegians I had dealt with. He tried his best to help me and made sure his sketchy English was understood before starting a new sentence. I sat with him on the bus and we chatted about the village and the weather; it was a no-smoking bus, though, and every now and again I would step out into the freezing cold air and spark up a cigarette, each time having to enjoy the non-smoking driver's continual, gentle taunts. Non-smokers always seem to find mileage in the bemusement of smokers' addiction.

He eventually took a studied look at his watch and said, "Come on, we're going now." He ground into gear and off through the snow and ice we slid, bound for the railway station. I there boarded the next train to Stockholm in the south-east of the country, a coastal, eastward-looking city situated where the Baltic meets the Gulf of Bothnia. It was a wondrous, white journey, with views as breathtaking as the air itself. Stockholm too is a satisfying place, a thriving, positive and picturesque city.

I was extremely tired, not having had any appreciable period of sleep for several days. Fortunately the people at the hotel I booked into asked no questions about identification and accepted pounds. The warmth of the room and the light pressure of the soft pillow against my head sent me into an instant, vitalising sleep. It had been an eventful few days.

Stockholm was never my intended destination, however. The next day I got up, picked up my indispensable luggage and made my way to Stockholm Central Station and boarded a train to Copenhagen, the capital city of Denmark. At one point the guard found me weeping in my seat, an embarrassing experience for both of us. As I have said, I was not the kind of person who cries, and certainly did not like people catching me in floods of tears. It was not part of my being, but once the smallest zephyr of emotion breathed into me, I was unstoppable. The tears kept coming, even when the guard had comforted me. My crying was beginning to get in the way of day-to-day life, but I could see no way of preventing it.

In Copenhagen I checked into a hotel, again staying one night. It was all very strange to me. I had no idea where I would eventually attempt to gain asylum; for the time being I was compelled merely to travel, almost aimlessly, from station to station, city to city, until I got a feel for somewhere. I was without a passport, without identification, and the pining for Omar was all the mental activity I could take.

During a rare period of emotional clarity, I sat down and tried to think logically about where to go next, where to stop. The idea of Germany hit me forcefully. I could speak German well enough to get by, so when the option finally occurred to me I wondered why I had never thought of it before. I was told I could catch a train from Copenhagen to Kiel, a reasonably large city in the north of Germany, 80 km south of the Danish border. Another night, another hotel.

On awaking in Kiel, I made my way to the station and placed my suitcase containing nearly all my money in a deposit box. I then sought out a police station and asked where I could make a claim for asylum. I was careful not to speak German, which was infuriating when they did not understand me, but communicating in English we managed to get our messages across. Speaking German would have aroused some suspicion, even in Germany, as it is quite well known that throughout most of the Middle East the only foreign languages taught in school are English and French; I would not have thought that many German-speaking asylum seekers presented themselves in the country. The address he gave me was of a place in Leipzig, 350 km to the south east. Another 350 km in the same direction and I would have been back in Vienna, making my travels of the previous few years into an enormous circle, but one I did not care to complete.

I retrieved my suitcase and caught the train to Leipzig, then locked the case up in another deposit box at the city's main station. At last, after days of travel, I made my way to the centre and declared that I wanted to claim asylum, again under an assumed identity – Ziad sounded convincing enough.

They took me in, but informed me that I would not be able to remain in Leipzig, that I would need to stay in yet another refugee camp in eastern Germany. That meant another trip to the station, and a change of scenery for my suitcase, which was by now almost rolling to the deposit boxes itself.

The asylum centre comprised three buildings, each of five storeys. I am told that their original use was as barracks for the Russian military during Germany's divided Cold War days. A clean-shaven, bespectacled Latif, alias

Ziad, took about a hundred dollars out of the suitcase and went to the reception to claim asylum. The receptionist looked up at me and simply said, "Go in." Inside was an office. I made my claim there. The staff were not unpleasant, but were methodical and helpful. I was fingerprinted during my induction, and a translator was provided. He was quite clearly Kurdish. The moment he found out I was from Baghdad his mood visibly sank, an indication of the enmity that is seemingly unaffected by distance. Once he found out I was an Arabic Baghdadi, rather than a Kurdish one, well that was it, I could be assured of no favours from him.

I was speaking in Arabic, and he was translating between German and Arabic. Of course, he was not to know that I had lived in a germanophone country, so he quite reasonably thought he could get away with translating everything I said either with a negative feel to it or completely wrongly, in order to give the officials the worst possible picture of me. I wondered how often had he done this to other Baghdadis he had taken a dislike to. But I could say nothing about it – I could not betray my past.

I looked the translator in the eye, and in Arabic, said, "Listen. I know what you're saying to them. Start translating me faithfully or I'll tell them exactly what you're doing, and you'll be out of a job, my friend."

"You speak German?" he gasped.

"No, but I understand it a bit. I can tell when you're making things up. Just start translating me properly."

The meeting over, I signed a few sheets of paper and was taken to the camp proper, on the second floor of one of the buildings. The room was large, and each contained eight single beds. Each bed had its own bedside cabinet, lamp and wardrobe. There was not a great deal of privacy but it was clean and tidy, and must have been a welcome change to many of those whose journey here had been less physically comfortable than my own.

Also present at the camp were many Kurds. The different factions were kept apart, and for good reason: whenever Jalal Talabani and Massoud al-Barzani had one of their turf battles in the American-controlled area of north Iraq, the inhabitants of the asylum centre would rise against each other, as surely as a D note sounding will make a D string on a nearby guitar hum, seemingly spontaneously. These battles in Kurdistan had nothing to do with Saddam. The idea that the region is and was a united front, poised to assist in the overthrow of Saddam, is a myth – there was as much ideological and territorial variation among them as there was between them and the ruling factions in Baghdad.

Baghdadis and people of other nationalities had a building to themselves. The second building was devoted to Massoud al-Barzani's supporters, the third to Jalal Talabani's. It was a situation not unlike that seen in prisons in Northern Ireland during the Troubles – except that this was not a prison.

I was thankfully housed with the Baghdadis. From day one my room-mates started insulting me, but always with smiles on their faces. There is a bond between people of the city, and insults are rarely heartfelt – it is merely a way of breaking down barriers and showing friendliness. They smiled whenever I could invent a suitably offensive jibe at their expense. Several of my neighbours became my friends through this unusual banter.

"How long does it normally take to get asylum here?" I asked one of my friends.

"Oh, a week or two, usually," he replied.

After I had been there a week, inter-factional conflict restarted in the north of Iraq. As expected, the disharmony of the battles resonated in our camp, and the occupants of the two buildings quite literally went to war with each other. There were knives and all manner of weapons being thrust and thrown between the warring parties, and the scene descended into a bloodbath, with mutilated bodies slumped all over the camp and the injured screaming and dragging themselves away. The Baghdadis were neither targeted nor forced to join in. Before long the place was awash with riot police and ambulances, and the violence slowly receded. Things had reached the stage were the emergency services had to keep an eye on developments in Kurdistan in order to prepare for the near certainty of a pitched battle erupting in the camp echoing any disquiet in Iraq. Two weeks later, I was granted asylum – again under a false name. When people are granted asylum in Germany, they become entitled to small regular payments and their accommodation is paid for by the state. I had to go along with this formality, even though I did not feel like I needed the money. All I was interested in was getting some official documentation so that I could start a business and earn a living. For the time being, however, I would have to stay at the camp.

Two days after asylum was granted, two police officers, one male and one female, and a translator came into my room at the camp and asked me to accompany them. We walked through to an office and sat down. They talked amongst themselves light-heartedly and shuffled papers around. I assumed I was about to be relocated.

"So," one of them began, "we see you have successfully been granted asylum."

"Yes," I nodded, "that's true."

"The trouble is, we have found that you were not long ago in Norway, and we know it was you because we ran a fingerprint match. You were there under a false name, and you have come to Germany and given another false identity. And we also have information that you are Latif Yahia, the double of Saddam Hussein's son, Uday."

I could see something in the Kurdish translator's eyes – he was fuming, burning with hatred, and failing dismally to hide it, even though he was continuing to write on a form. He must not have heard about the news until that moment.

"Stop," I shouted, "before you go on, I want this translator out of the room."
"So who will translate?"

"Ich spreche Deutsch," I said, then reiterated my desire for the translator to be removed from the room. He was sent out. I continued talking, in German: "For my security—"

The woman interrupted. "Wow! You speak German very well!"
"Thank you," I smiled. "I lived in Austria for a while. I also lived in England, in Norway. I want to kill Latif Yahia. He is a liability."

"No problem," she said. "We will refer your story to the Department of Justice, and in a day or two you will be transferred to a safe place." I have to say I felt safe in their care. The international reputation of the clinical, precise nation might be true of their prowess in engineering, but in day-to-day life I find the Germans a warm, humorous and generous people. "It will be a maximum of two days, I'm sure. We understand the depth of feeling between the central Iraqis and the Kurds, and yours is a special case," she concluded. Then her tone softened. "My God, Latif, your book is brilliant! As soon as we found out who you were I made sure I got a copy and it has barely left my hand ever since." She reached into her handbag and pulled out Ich war Saddams Sohn, and asked me to sign it. With a flourish of my wrist and a grin on my embarrassed face, I autographed her copy. Shaking my hand, she said, "Look, if you need anything, here is my number." She gave me both her official phone number and her personal mobile number.

I set off for my room feeling happy. But what I had not counted on was that the translator had broken the news of my identity to everyone he had stumbled upon, and by now the entire camp was aware – and at least two-thirds of them wanted my head on a pike. Since it was daytime, the police and guards were out in force, so my walk back to my block was a tense but effectively safe one. As I walked, people stopped what they were doing and stared at me. I had undergone a change of appearance by shaving and wearing glasses, but it was clear that they were in their minds drawing back the beard, turning my spectacles into sunglasses, fitting me out in an Italian suit and inflicting a swagger on my gait. By the time I arrived at my block, there was no doubt in anyone's mind that I was Latif Yahia; it is at times like this that one needs a double. As far as they were concerned, I was a willing, adopted member of the Tikriti clan. In their minds, I must have volunteered to be Uday's fiday, been a loyal party member and was therefore an instrument of their oppression. There would have been no point trying to explain the truth to them; as soon as the Kurdish translator had started spreading the story, my fate was sealed – they would never believe an Arab over a Kurd, no matter how much Kurdish blood coursed through my veins.

The bars and restaurants in the town started filling as evening began to creep towards the camp; many of the diners would have been guards and police officers. There was a visible reduction in the numbers on patrol, and with that came a tangible shift in the mood.

"Be careful, Latif," warned my Baghdadi friends, ceaselessly. "The Kurds are all mad. They will try something, for sure." They could, I thought, sense something in the air. Perhaps it was the stirring they had experienced many times before and had learnt to interpret as the overboiling of one of the Kurds' interfactional frays. For now at least, it seemed, the Kurds were united by a common enemy: me.

"I should be okay," I said. "They say I'll be out in a day or two."

They looked at each other uneasily. This confirmed to me that they could definitely sense something much closer to home. "We hope so," one said, "but until then do not leave this room. Don't even go for food. We'll bring it up here for you."

I nodded warily.

At eleven, we locked ourselves into our room from the inside and started settling down for the night. But a terrific crash made everyone bolt. The door had been kicked off its hinges and it slammed against the floor. And there, on the outside were dozens of Kurds, each one of them darting his eyes around the room, looking for me. On making visual contact with their target, they burst through the doorway, and we then saw that they were armed with knives, chair legs or whatever weapon they could fashion or get hold of. What is more, every one of them was drunk; some of them could barely stand, while others were intoxicated to the point of psychosis. Any hope of reasoning with these people already seemed lost. All of us in the room stiffened with terror.

Shouting rose up all around the room – cries for help merging with battle cries and gut-wrenching curses. The first person they reached they picked up and threw out of the window. He fell two storeys to his death. The murdering had begun, and if anyone thought they had come just to scare us they were at that moment stunned into defensive action. Fists and other weapons flew wildly in every direction, and jets of blood squirted from the wounds on both sides. The sickening, dull snapping of limbs and the cries of anguish punctuated the background screams of horror and hatred.

It was me they were after, though, and they started to get close. Did the Baghdadis run away and leave me to my fate? No, they crowded around me and took the blows of the frenzied mass of Kurdish murderers. Like wasps protecting their queen from an attacking predator, they instinctively put themselves between the Kurds and me, then started to edge towards the door. I took a few painful hits, but compared to some of those protecting me I got off extremely lightly. There is no room for debate here – those Baghdadis saved my life that night. The Kurds would have killed me and danced on my body.

Forty or fifty police cars arrived, sirens howling; two helicopters with spot-lights hovered overhead. What they must have been able to see below them must have been shocking. The attempt to murder me was eventually quelled with force. Dozens were injured and I have no idea how many were killed; convoys of ambulances took victims to hospital.

My injuries required only two stitches; most of the heroic men who stood around me were coming out of casualty with twenty or more. Shock and pain was gouged into every face. All I could feel was relief and a deep guilt and gratitude for the ones who had been killed or injured.

I was taken to a safe house two hours' drive from the camp; it was a pleasant and comfortable place in a bucolic setting, with a small village centre housing a handful of shops. My neighbours were Hungarians and Yugoslavs. Every moment of my stay there I was under watertight police guard. They offered to get me anything I wanted, and looked after me without complaint or sideways glance. They also provided me with reassurance, something that was invaluable to me at the time.

They never brought up the fact that I had given a false name or asked me about my past. Like the Norwegians had done, they fully understood my motives, and any leverage they could have gained by dangling this in front of me was never so much as hinted at. It was like being a human being again, and treated with the respect and individuality that had been missing from my life since I was at university.

I do not know if diplomatic exchanges took place between Norway and Germany. I suppose there must have been, as I was not extradited. I was, of course, a wanted man in Norway, and a bail-jumper at that. I must have been made a special case, or perhaps the German authorities were better equipped to deal with me.

To the German police, the authorities and the citizens, and to my room-mates in the camp, I owe not just my gratitude, but my every breathing day on this earth.

A serious problem existed, and to a degree still exists, in the Kurdish region, and it was a major factor in the events described in this chapter. It derived from the fact that the majority of Kurds were uneducated peasants and simply followed whichever leader offered them the best deal. Many of them had never strayed outside the valley they were born in; a good deal had never set eyes on a city, let alone people from a culture different to their own. They were the perfect patsies for the warlords and bandits who could get them on their side by offering them money and weaponry. They would soon be brainwashed into believing that they were under threat from all sides. Joining a Peshmerga group would afford them protection and status; they rarely joined for ideological reasons, as they had no access to the requisite education. Their faction became their family and for this they would fight and die.

Certain factions controlled the oil which passed through the North of Iraq bound for Turkey. They would set up checkpoints and charge tanker drivers $300 to pass through a $600 return trip. The leaders became rich on the proceeds as a couple of thousand tankers would make the trip each day 365 days a year, and when southern factions started to make demands that the money be split between all Kurds equitably, small wars would erupt. These were the kinds of pointless interfactional episodes over which the Kurds in Germany would feel lethal affinity.

During the time Saddam was at his oppressive worst in the Kurdish lands, very few sought asylum. They lived through the atrocities, including the terrible gas attack in Halabja, but remained in place. It was not until the Americans occupied the territories that they started to flee the region in their droves. Any Kurd could mention their origin in an asylum interview and be practically assured a favourable decision. Before long there were millions dotted around Europe.

It is interesting that Turkish Kurds, equally as oppressed as the Iraqi ones, receive little sympathy. They are not even allowed to speak their own language.

Could it be because Turkey is a member of NATO?

When the Peshmerga groups are not at each other's throats, they can agree on one thing – that they want independence from Iraq and Turkey. This opinion comes with one stipulation: that the oil-rich city of Kirkuk is part of the deal. Without the oil, they care little for independence. Of course, it is not the peasants and farmers who would benefit from such an arrangement, it is the very people who have indoctrinated them to fight for their cause. Should an independent state of Kurdistan ever become a political reality, it would take a miracle to prevent it descending into civil war as each of the factions, armed by the West, fought over oilfields, the proceeds from which would go straight over their heads.

The educated among the Iraqi Kurds realise this. They go one of two ways: either they support the continuation of the Kurdish area's being a part of

Iraq, playing a role in its prosperity and its place in the world as a civilised democracy; or they try to get together an army of people hitherto indifferent to anything beyond their own families and valleys, and make them fight for their leaders' selfish desire to control the oil and to install their own families as virtual monarchies, replacing the overthrown clan from Tikrit with another. The former group of educated Kurds is large and provide some hope. However, the rabble-rousers always shout the loudest. (Many of the warlords were, at the time of writing this book, early in 2005, representing Kurdish voters in the Iraqi parliament. Rural Kurds have little experience of politics, and on the whole voted for the tribal leader that they were instructed to. One of the first laws passed by the interim government was that dual nationality would be permitted. This allowed the leaders to continue their money-siphoning activities – donations from the west run into the billions – and no doubt flee Iraq when they have taken all they want. That is, of course, unless a separate Kurdish state starts to look like a possibility. Jalal Talabani, who was one of those controlling oil in the north, became Iraq's President in 2005. Nechirvan Barzani, who the Kurds used to call "The Kurdish Uday" because of the way he acted and dressed, and because of his indulgent, violent, playboy lifestyle, became the leader of the Kurdish parliament. He happens also – by coincidence, no doubt – to be the nephew of Massoud Barzani. There is a dangerous lack of real political education in the region, and unless action is taken, the whole area will explode, or set in motion an aristocracy that will become impossible to dislodge. Does that sound familiar?)

- Chapter 8 -
The Voice at the Back
of my Head

Between July and August 1996 I lived under German protection – and it was protection, not custody – in my safe house in this quiet, unimposing village. It was another month of tears.

During the days there were plenty of diversions to keep my mind active and focused on the present and, I dared, the future. But as soon as night-time approached and the peacefulness of the village turned to an absolute silence where even the birds in the trees relaxed and stopped singing, my past and my dear family would wander back into my present. They were right there, their individual laughs, voices and mannerisms, and yet it was impossible to talk to them, to touch them, to feel their warmth. The photograph I had of my son started to wear at the edges through the frequency and tightness with which I would grip it. Where is he? Was he cold? Was he hungry? Was he smiling? Was life being kind to him? Was he even alive? Tara was that little bit older, and yet I feared for her, too. I loved her as I still do, because I helped to raise her from infancy and because as far as she was concerned, I was her father. Always in the back of my mind, however, was the knowledge that one day Nusa and I would inevitably split, and that when that day came, Tara would be holding her hand, not mine. It is possible that a deeply rooted sense of detachment was present, but it did not affect how much paternal love I had for her. Who could have resisted that tiny, stick-limbed girl toddling towards me at the airport, her sweet little face alight with excitement, shouting "Baba! Baba!" with all her strength?

I was probably grieving for my father, too; the news, when it had been broken to me, went straight to the department of my mind dealing with anger and despair, not the part that allowed the grief to flood out and purify the soul and to allow me to accept my new, fatherless, reality. I was not through with my father. We still had much to say, many experiences to share. I imagine anyone who is bereaved through a sudden illness or accident feels the same helplessness and sense of being left in mid-air, trying to ease away from the relationship that still feels so alive. But a murder was that much more disturbing, because it was a purposeful, human act, and therefore as avoidable as it is deplorable. Whoever poisoned my father could have changed his mind at the last minute; it could have been that close, that black and white. The life of a human being – my father, no less – was probably ended by a tactical decision. And that is almost impossible to come to terms with.

Oftentimes I did not know why I was crying. I would look into the mirror at the streams of tears rolling down my face and wonder what was making them all come, and tried to imagine when they would stop. But no end was in sight; indeed, it felt like the feelings were still getting worse with each passing hour.

There was also the relentless, boiling rage inside me sparked by what Nusa had done. She had millions of pounds and dollars that were rightfully mine, even though the money would have become hers had I been killed. But I was still alive. I felt like I had done so much for her, helping her to escape and looking after her once we did. We even became intimate, yet time and again she would repay me with lies, betrayal, hatred and manic outbursts. And now she had turned to nothing less than kidnap to prove whatever point it was she was trying to make. I did not own her. I am not some Saudi prince who expects absolute loyalty from my partner in return for a life of comfortable boredom. We had an arrangement which was working well enough and at no point was she not free to leave. But the way she left, and what and whom she took with her, was unforgivable. I needed to track her down, but was struggling to find a way to do it while maintaining my anonymity. In the absence of any hope of getting my father back, this would at least be a step in the right direction. It would help me, give me something to aim at, become my project. In addition to all the mental turbulence playing with my mind, I felt a powerful sense of embarrassment that I had tried to enter this country on false pretences. Germany and its people had looked after me unquestioningly; they had trusted, housed, protected and respected me. And what had I done in return? Cheated on them. Although the authorities assured me that they fully understood the reasons behind my actions, I could barely look any of their personnel in the face. As children we are all caught with our hands in the biscuit tin when we have promised not even to open it. It is a betrayal of trust that can trigger an overflowing explosion of shame. Multiply that by a thousand, and you come close to how I felt at every meeting with them, formal or informal.

There was also a pragmatic element to my embarrassment, however: would they ever again believe a word I said? Did they consider me trustworthy, this man who had sat through interviews with an Arabic translator, listening to each sentence twice, sometimes in edited form, and not let them into my secret? I thought not. From then on, they would have to think twice about my every assertion, and make an educated judgement as to whether I was lying or telling the truth. Sometimes they would be wrong, and I could lose out in this high-stakes game of chance. At that moment I decided to emigrate.

I cleared a space on the living room floor and rolled out my dog-eared map of Europe. It was beginning to look very familiar. Where now?

The name of another haven jumped up at me: The Netherlands. I had visited Holland for television interviews, on business and had even taken a couple of short holidays there, and had always found the place tolerant and friendly. And if there is a city on earth more delightful than Amsterdam, I am sure I would by now have at least heard of it. Of course, living there is very different from visiting. There is a whole array of new laws to master, new financial situations to come into line with, a new language to master, and innumerable cultural traits and taboos to become versed in. But it had to be worth a try. I had already made up my mind that I could not stay in Germany, so in my mind I was descending onto Europe from space, and simply had to steer myself in the right direction.

I did not feel that I could tell the police or the authorities I was leaving. I needed to arrive in Amsterdam incognito, and I wanted to remain untraceable. So without mentioning it to anybody in authority, I called a taxi and asked the driver to take me to the nearest railway station from where I could get a train to Holland.

"You know we are in the east of Germany, don't you?" he said. "The Holland-bound trains all leave from the west. It would be an expensive ride."

Déjà vu hit me as I told the driver to name his price and that I would pay it. We struck a deal and he duly took me and all my possessions to the station. Again, all the potentials of a new country at once turned into more practical matters.

Before I left, I wrote the German authorities a letter retracting my claim for asylum, and telling them that I was grateful for all they had done but that I did not feel safe and wanted to move on. Naturally, I left them guessing about the destination. I posted it as we were leaving the village. (An Amsterdam postmark might have given the game away.) I had never felt duty bound to do this on any of the other occasions when I had decided to abscond from a country. There must have been some sort of affection playing on my mind; the letter began, "By the time you get this letter I will be gone …" or words to that effect. It was effectively the end of a relationship. But after all the misfortunes that had surrounded me since I arrived in Germany – none of it, I hasten to add, the fault of the Germans – I was reasonably happy to be on the move once again.

There followed another train journey – a short one, compared to those I had taken over the previous months. My cash-packed suitcase and I arrived in the vibrant and stimulating city of Amsterdam with new hope. I checked into one of the city's luxurious hotels, and stayed there for about ten days, which gave me plenty of time to think and plan for the future, and to decide whether or not the Dutch lifestyle was for me. Who was I kidding? It is an enviable lifestyle. I opted to stay, if possible with full asylum, or even citizenship.

One beneficial aspect of hotels is that the occupants normally have only one key, so there are no sets to jangle and set my heart racing. The downside was that I got used to not hearing the dreaded sound, so on the rare occasions when I did, such as the night my neighbour locked herself out of her room and had to be let in by the hotel staff, I would jump doubly violently. Those keys still had me locked away from a normal life.

The next day, I followed my suitcase to the nearest railway station deposit box, locked it inside, then set about buying a few unstylish clothes and visiting wherever the locals processed asylum claims, posing as a penniless refugee named anything other than Latif Yahia. I made my way to the police station.

"I would like to claim asylum," I declared in English to the policeman behind the desk.

"No problem," he said, in perfect English. "You are welcome, but we don't process claims in Amsterdam." He wrote down the address for me and told me that the place was about two hours away by train. They gave me a free train ticket; again, I could not divulge the fact that I had a suitcase full of money. I really did feel welcome. Even better, nobody recognised me. Things were looking good. I was playing it by the book, so only a bizarre incident could stop this from going through.

During my stay in the hotel I had made friends with a Moroccan, and we became close enough for him to let slip what his line of work was – he forged passports. He must have sensed in me an itinerant streak.

"Just say the word," he had laughed, "and I can get you a brand new Dutch passport. Three and a half thousand guilders."

I was interested but cautious. A forged passport would be very useful for me if I ever had the need to leave a country quicker than the proper channels would allow, particularly if I was refused asylum here. "Before I hand over my money, do you have any proof about what you say you can do?" I asked. "You don't need to give me any money," he replied. "Pay me when you get it. If you get no passport, you pay nothing. If you're not happy with it, you pay nothing."

"Okay," I said. I paid a visit to the photo booth to have a photograph of myself taken. Straight away I gave it to him, and the following day he knocked on my hotel door bearing a very realistic forgery. Of course, it was not made out in my real name – I wanted that part of me to be consigned to history. I handed over the money and never saw him again.

After releasing my suitcase from the deposit box, travelling to the town where the asylum processing office was located, and locking the case up again, I reported to the office wearing my worst, dirtied tee-shirt and jeans and carrying a plastic bag containing a change of clothes. This was my interview suit. I should run a night school course on asylum seeking, I thought. Lesson one: Acting the part. Lesson two: Exposing hostile interpreters.

There was a large gate with a small door next to it. I knocked on the door and was let in. The reception hall was clean and the staff appeared hospitable, which always helps put the mind at ease when entering such a place. At the reception I spoke in English, and they answered me in English. Unlike the Austrian system, which seemed to be designed to put people off claiming, the Dutch asylum process had evidently been engineered to speed up the process and to give the refugee a fair hearing, as well as to improve the lot of some of the world's most vulnerable people. By their obstinacy, the Austrians were of course making more work for themselves, and since they had an international obligation to accept asylum seekers, their system could reasonably be thought of as self-defeating. Nobody would deny that there is a need for screening people entering a country, as the asylum route has been a convenient cover for many a criminal on the run; and jumping the queue for normal immigration by attempting to defraud the asylum system is selfish and creates suspicion and detestation of genuine refugees. But there is no justification in treating all asylum seekers as guilty of deception until proven otherwise; it is neither humane nor constructive, and national reputations for ill-treatment are hard to shake off.

"Welcome," said the representative, shaking my hand. "What language do you speak?"

"Arabic," I replied.

"Well we're sorry, but you will have to wait about half an hour for the translator. We hope you don't mind."

"Of course not," I said, and sat down in a waiting area. Others entering the room were treated equally as professionally.

After a short wait I was asked to accompany a member of staff to the interview room, where a few officials and a translator awaited me. I was dismayed to see that the translator was Kurdish – are there no Arabic Arabic translators in the European asylum system? At least one of the translators I had encountered, the one in Germany, did have a reasonable grasp of German but his Arabic was, I found, inaccurate and misleading even when he was not trying to deceive the staff.

We sat down and I found out that the interview was to be a preliminary one just to get a few basic facts together. I was to stay at the camp that night and my interview proper would be the next day. They would also try to find me some more permanent housing, but in the meantime I would be accommodated in another camp.

The preliminary interview over, I was taken to the living quarters. It was a large, comfortable place but I was not allowed to smoke in the bedroom and had to go outside for a cigarette. I found this reasonable enough, although to a nicotine addict, as I had become, it meant lots of annoying trips outside. Also, the doors were closed at 8 p.m., so there were to be no visits to the all-night supermarket for me.

The food was good and the people were very pleasant; I started to think that Austria was the exception rather than the rule when it came to treating inmates like farm animals, even though the experience had shaped my opinions on what refugee camps were like. The ratio of the origins of the asylum seekers in The Netherlands was roughly the same as that in

Germany: it was about two-thirds Kurdish. They seem to be everywhere but Kurdistan.

The next day my name was called – or at any rate the name I had given them – and I made my way to another block where the interview would take place. The interview room was pleasantly informal and comfortable. Along a stretched desk were three police interviewers, one civilian and the same translator as the previous day, all with their papers and files in front of them. Officialdom was at a minimum. The place was decorated and furnished not unlike someone's living room – there were potted houseplants and pictures, and there was even a small television set behind me which remained switched on during the interview but with the sound turned low.

The interview started formally, however, with my name and other details being given. I was well into my life story, or the one I had composed for myself, the one where I had been smuggled out of Iraq a few weeks ago and brought here stuffed into the suffocating cubby-holes of various lorries. Notes were being taken and things were going well. So far, so good. After five minutes I realised that the man in the middle of the five was not really paying attention to what I or any of his colleagues on the panel were saying. He was looking straight past me, a baffled expression on his face. In an instant he stopped everyone from talking by leaping up and pointing at me with one hand and gesticulating with the other. "Are you sure you left Iraq only recently?" he demanded. He was visibly excited.

"Yes" I said calmly, through my teeth.

"Positive?" he said.

"Yes," I repeated, although by now even I was wondering if my story was true. He turned to his colleagues and nodded at the television behind me. The translator looked between it and me as though he were a spectator at a tennis match. Within seconds a realisation had dawned on all of them. Amusement, surprise and puzzlement resulted.

"Look," said one, "we know who you are."

"What do you mean," I asked, innocently.

"Stand up," another said.
I stood up.

"Now look at the TV."

I turned round, and saw none other than Latif Yahia, being interviewed on TRUS TV. It was the interview I had done several years earlier in 1994, not long after I had been freed from the Austrian prison. I was in full flow, criticising everyone and attempting to set some heads rolling. I looked young, optimistic and relatively healthy, despite the traumas I had escaped from not long before. The intervening years had drained me of much of my youthfulness. But not enough to get me out of this predicament.

"Now tell me: Who is that on the TV?" asked one of the interviewers – rhetorically, I feel.

A spontaneous grimace stretched my face. "Fuck!" I exclaimed, bowing my head and shaking it. Naturally I thought they had used some incredible detective skills to get hold of this interview with me in time for my interview. But it was not as complicated as that. It was a mere coincidence, an unbelievable, uncanny, breathtakingly shitty coincidence. A repeat broadcast, for whatever reason, but one which had torpedoed my chances of pulling off an asylum attempt under my assumed name. I turned back to face the interviewers with the widest of smiles on my face, and my voice broke in to laughter as I said, "My God, am I unlucky? Why today? Why now? I can't believe it! Is this on now or is it a video?"

"It's on now," one of them replied. "And yes, it appears that you are the victim of an amazing coincidence."

They were as amused by the coincidence as I was, except for the Kurdish translator, who could not hide his emotions: he was seething in anger and hatred and could not see the funny side at all.

I stopped myself laughing to make sure the staff knew I was being absolutely serious. "Please," I said. "I want the translator out of the interview. I want to talk to you in private about something he must not hear."

He was asked to leave, and when he was out of earshot, one of the interviewers stood and said, "Latif Yahia, welcome to Holland! You are a special case now. We are not authorised to make any decisions without first contacting the Department of Justice. Please give me ten minutes – I'll go and call them now." He left the room.

"Do you want to smoke?" I was asked. "Or do you want anything else?"

"Please," I replied, "I want a coffee and a smoke." I was still in a state of bewilderment at what had happened.

"There is no smoking allowed in here," I was told. "Come on, we'll go to the officers' quarters." We went to the place where the police who staffed the camp had their meals and took breaks. It was another comfortable room, and I was given cigarettes, coffee and biscuits. "Don't worry," I was reassured, "you are not like normal cases. You will be treated differently."

"Thank you very much," I said with a nod. But already too many people knew my identity, most alarmingly for me the Kurdish translator, who would no doubt already have been in touch with his compatriots and other contacts telling them of my whereabouts. I did not want a repeat of the German camp incident. I had had enough of repeats already today.

After an hour and a half in the mess room, the secretary of the minister of justice arrived. We shook hands. "Welcome to Holland," he said. "I hope you will make Holland your country. We honestly think nothing of the fact that you lied to us and realise why you did it, so please do not worry about it. We won't even treat it as a lie."

I thanked him and told him all about the unfortunate events that had blighted my life over the previous months – about having all my possessions taken, losing my children while I was in prison, the riot in Germany, and everything else besides. He seemed genuinely concerned about me.

"As I said," he concluded, "please do not worry. Your troubles are over now. You will be able to stay here tonight, and you will be sleeping not with the refugees, but with the police. Tomorrow we will put you somewhere safe." This could not happen. I had to be completely straight with the secretary. "Can I just say something," I said. "Thank you for coming, and my regards and respect go to this country and to the people of this country. It's just that I feel so guilty to you now for lying to you." It was true. I felt exactly as I had done in Germany. It might seem reprehensible that the guilt only hit me when I had been caught, and not while I was benefiting from the countries' kindness, but in my defence I would say that I had never had the intention of using my true identity to benefit from the countries; as soon as my new identity was assured, I was all set to blend into the background and start afresh. My guilt came from the fact that the people who had been so kind to me might well have felt like I was playing a game with them, trying to make myself appear superior while they were disposable pawns, tools of my dishonest trade. In having my identity revealed, I felt as though I had created a set of innocent victims, which would not have been the case had I got away with it. Perhaps they would be passed over when promotion or other career-enhancing opportunities surfaced. Whichever way you look at it, my actions had not benefited those who were about to look after me.

"Don't worry!" the secretary repeated. "We accept that it's because of your security. We know you've been threatened and that your life is in danger. Please don't think we will hold it against you. Don't forget, your book was published in Holland, you've been on our TV … as I'm sure you don't need reminding. You are very welcome here. We are flattered that someone like you – a political refugee with such a genuinely horrifying story – should choose our country as your place of refuge."

I shook my head. "Thank you, but I still feel really, really guilty. I can't stay here."

"Where are you going to go?" he asked.

"Am I under arrest here?" I returned.

"No, no," he said, waving his hands at me and shaking his head. "Nobody arrested you. You are free to go and free to stay. Just consider our offer. We'll find you a really nice, safe place where nobody will know who you are. We'll change your identity."

I shook my head shamefully, then looked up at the secretary and said, "Thank you, but no. I feel so, so guilty. Please, can I leave?"

"Where would you go?" he again demanded.

"Please," I said, "I'm not under arrest. I am very grateful for what you have done for me, but I will not tell you where I'm going. Just believe me, I'm going to leave this country as soon as I can."

He looked back at me and said, "Okay. I can't force you to do anything. Let me just say that you are welcome here any time you want to come." He shook my hand and guided me out of the building. "Do you have a car?" He asked.

"Please," I stressed, "you're very kind, but just let me go. I'll be fine."

"Do you at least want a lift somewhere? There are no taxis around here."

I gave in and accepted a lift to the railway station. I was driven in a procession of two unmarked police cars, both of which had in them several policemen. A few of them were dressed as though they were quite highly ranked, I imagine for the security of the secretary rather than for me. When they dropped me off they got out of their cars and one by one shook me by the hand and wished me good luck. I was surrounded by well-wishing policemen, making quite a spectacle at the station. I could see the other passengers' puzzled expressions as they plundered their memories to put a name to my face. The police tried to insist on staying with me until I caught my train but I eventually persuaded them to leave me to myself. I must say I got very embarrassed, but I am sure it was all done with the best intentions. And besides, I had a suitcase to pick up.

Within the hour I was sitting on a train back to Amsterdam with a confusion of images flying through my head. I had really thought that Holland was the place in which I could settle down. I had set my heart on it, and for a while that dream had filled me with a positivity otherwise absent in my life. It was difficult to accept that all my carefully laid plans had come to nothing thanks to a ridiculous freak event.

On arrival back at the hotel I got out my map of Europe again, and sighed as I surveyed the differently coloured territories marked on it. "Fuck!" I whispered to myself. "Where can I go that I haven't already been?" Most of northern and central Europe was out of the question. And Iceland sounded a little too chilly for my Middle-Eastern constitution, even though I had experienced Tundra living the previous winter.

Beyond the United Kingdom, however, was a place I had of course heard of but knew very little about – Ireland.

I made a trip to the travel agent. "Will I need a visa to go to Ireland?" I enquired.

"What passport do you have?"

"Dutch," I replied, and showed her my forgery.

"Then no, you won't need a passport," she replied. "Ireland is an EU Member State."

"Great," I said. "So can I have a ticket to Dublin?"

"Of course," she smiled. "Just give me your passport and I'll sort everything out."

Thanks to the mastery of the forgers, she did not suspect for a second that the passport was a fake. This cheered me, for obvious reasons. Within minutes I had a plane ticket to Dublin.

By that point I was too wily to be full of hope. Ireland has quite a large area for its population, however, with most of the Irish living in the couple of major cities – as I saw it, one of the cities must have been able to provide a good opportunity to blend in and disappear.

I needed time to sit still and to consider my sanity, repair my constitution and begin to clamber back up to a state of financial security. I also had to locate Omar and Tara, which would mean tracking down Nusa – a daunting task epitomised. There was also the matter of Uday and how I could play my part in his downfall.

With a case of cash and a mind full of plans, I arrived in Dublin on 2 December 1997.

*   *   *   *   *

The idea to write this story came to me a year or so after leaving prison in Austria. I thought it would be interesting to chronicle my experiences of Austrian justice and the life of an asylum seeker, albeit one with an extraordinary story and a best-selling book behind him. I thought it would make a good newspaper feature or magazine article. But as events unfolded, and my personal life became the source of much anguish as well as joy, and as an accumulation of assassination attempts, murders and efforts to turn me into a murderer and a spy sent me deeper into despair than I had ever thought possible, it became obvious that I had another book in me, although it was difficult to decide on a point at which it would reach a conclusion.

I started to gather ideas, but events kept taking over and diverting me from writing or making me push the end-point of my story forward a few months. In Ireland my note-taking began in earnest, just as it had done secretly during the stultifying days in Uday's palace half a decade earlier. Naively I thought that my arrival in Ireland would precede the final full stop at the end of the book.

But my life never seems to be that simple or predictable.

What happened to me in the famously welcoming, cheery Emerald Isle at times made my experiences on mainland Europe look like a holiday. I could never have imagined how it could have been possible, but my darkest, lowest days were yet to come. My trip from The Netherlands to Ireland now seems to me to be an appropriate place to end this part of the story. The rest will have to wait for another book.

*   *   *   *   *

The chapters of this book have at times been painful and difficult to recall. The chronological nature of the narrative was difficult to stick to, as every story within it was either the trunk or a twig of a great, old tree, each one bringing forward a branch or a limb of explanation, be it background or subsequent events. It was not until I sat down at the computer and started typing that I realised the complexity and interweaving nature of the parts, and hope I have not caused too much confusion at the loom.

I have met hundreds of characters, some murderous, some greedy, some bent on my personal failure; others, of course, were loving, caring and honest. Even though Baghdad was a relatively modern city, in Europe I always felt like I was being thrown into a completely new culture and that I had to make my own way with the minimum of outside assistance, and later, completely alone. I entered Europe with nothing but the clothes I wore, and left its mainland with little more. In between I experienced wealth and poverty. I have been thrown into prisons and hob-nobbed with presidents, kings, diplomats and exiles. I have appeared on national television and in newspapers and magazines, and tried to secrete myself in deserted villages and the sprawling metropolis. It was a period of extremes and of contrasts. Most of it was spent without a plan, indeed not daring to make any plans, and simply living an ad hoc life, each day hoping the bullet or car bomb would not simultaneously greet me and wave me goodbye.

I am not proud of the way I broke the law and abused people's trust. False passports, dishonest asylum claims and violent outbursts are not features of my life that I would hope to pass on to my children, and I feel they will not exactly endear me to the general public. But in my way I hope I can justify every action, even if the justification was ephemeral and jaded by anger and resentment. I was without a nationality, and the one state that accepted me as Latif Yahia treated me abysmally. I could see no point in trying to carry on the legitimate life, and craved anonymity, particularly after the assassination attempts. I am reassured by the reactions of the German, Dutch and Norwegian authorities when my true identity was revealed; they understood how much danger I was in. As for the violence, I believe I was driven to it, and that my actions were usually taken on the spur of the moment. In my darker moments I still believe that the victims deserved what they got, but hope desperately that I am never again in the position to have to resort to such measures. I would find it very difficult to face Kessler again and not feel the pain surging through my body. However I feel I am now much better equipped to deal with anger, and have developed an intense dislike of violence of any kind.

Had I remained in Iraq, the details of this story might have been unremarkable, as what would be expected; Iraq was a violent place, a pariah in the eyes of the world, a country under the grip of a vicious and volatile regime which promised to remain in power perpetually, passing the leadership from father to son regardless of the will of the population. But I was not in Iraq. This was Europe, that beacon of civilised living, that standard-setter for every fledgling democracy that forces its way through the blood-soaked shell of tyranny. I was to find out that tyranny and democracy exist in symbiosis. A war-torn Middle East allows Western governments to assist, arm and prop up whichever regime offers them the best deal, and cheap oil, a comfortable life for the population and the electoral votes that follow naturally on. No matter what governments preach with superficial sincerity in public, behind the scenes they will be making life hell for countless oppressed souls.

In my tiny way I threatened to bring some of the truth to light. Hundreds of diligent activists all over Europe do a much better job than I could ever do at publicising the truths, but the message dawns on the public slowly. What I had to my advantage – or disadvantage, as it often transpired – was that I had been inside one of the world's most disgusting regimes. I had shaken hands with people who thought they were sealing illicit deals with the son of Saddam Hussein, Uday – a man for whom evil and abuses of power were parts of his everyday life and his personality. I have seen how many of those who are now very publicly "rebuilding" and "democratising" Iraq are little more than gangsters, hoarders and extortionists, whose political ambitions are only so fervent because of the personal, and potential hereditary, fortunes that can be had from it.

I think I am prepared for the backlash, for being brushed aside as a fanatic, an obsessive, even a liar. I believe that there are enough people out there who will take my words as what they are – the truth – and at the very least start to listen to their leaders' assertions with an open mind. Otherwise I would have maintained my life-preserving silence. Now that Baghdad is in the hands of not one clan but a set of clans, we shall see if leaving Saddam behind will have a healing effect on the country or if it will create a whole new set of problems.

Perhaps my story is Iraq's situation in microcosm. One might have imagined that the overthrowing and capture of Saddam would be the end of the Iraqi nightmare. But new surprises and disasters seem continually to be sprung upon the country and its population. It pains me to say this, but I happen to think that Iraq is about to have its hopes dashed once again, and that the long-anticipated release from Saddam, from Uday, from the generals and from the ministers will end up opening the doors to a crushing, depressing imprisonment at the hands of Western powers. It is difficult to see how the situation can be avoided without more bloodshed and suffering.

But on this subject, nothing would gratify me more than to be wrong.

- Postscript -

Is Austria a racist country? I found plenty of opportunities to ask myself that question during my stay there, and many more after I left. It is of course difficult to answer, and a conclusion in the negative or the affirmative would render me prone to accusations of making the kind of sweeping judgements that racists themselves indulge in. But, like asking if Saudi Arabia is a Muslim country, the question in truth seeks to find the direction in which the popular compass is pointing. One event might provide assistance in seeking which way Austria's collective mind thinks on the questions of nationalism, fascism and racism, and I shall attempt to describe it here.

While the world at large was preparing for, and recovering from, the turn of the millennium, Austria was undergoing a political change that was to put it at loggerheads with Europe and the wider world, and which made its complacent population analyse itself in a way that had seldom happened since 1945. The storm revolved around Jorg Haider, a populist politician who was the founder of Austria's right-wing Freedom Party. He had, almost a decade earlier, allegedly praised certain aspects of the Nazi character (a sentiment he would later retract), and despite various reforming actions had done little to shake off the Nazi image, even though he compared his party's policies with those of Tony Blair's.

Before the election of 1999, Haider was the governor of the southern Austrian province of Carinthia, but his political ambitions appeared to be greater when he took his party into the national governmental elections. The party stance was firmly right-wing and, to many, was inspired by Nazism; indeed, Haider came from a family with enthusiastic Nazi sympathies. The chief bugbear of the party was immigration: they wanted to halt it completely. The country, he opined, was overflowing with immigrants from Turkey, the former Soviet Union and the unstable Balkans, many of whom were seeking permanent residence, others asylum. The country's geographical position did not help matters: It borders the Czech Republic, Slovakia and Hungary and is a short journey from Turkey, Romania, Serbia, Bosnia and Croatia. He complained that Turks wanted to keep their own culture whilst living in Austria, rather than integrating, and that all those from the former Yugoslavia had to offer were crime, drug dealing and prostitution. He denied being inspired by racism, however, saying that immigrants who

Jorg Haide in Baghdad with Saddam

had lived in the country for twenty or thirty years (mainly Turks brought over to rebuild the shattered post-war infrastructure in a country with a severely depleted workforce) were welcome to stay, and that non-whites born in Austria to these people would also unquestioningly be accepted as his compatriots; he simply wanted immigration to stop. He went so far as to claim that his social policies, manifested in help for the disadvantaged in society, made him more of a socialist than a fascist. It was not clear how much this was a façade – albeit a pretty extreme one in itself – to find sympathy in a proportion of right-leaning voters who would not countenance putting a cross on a ballot paper next to an avowed Nazi, or whether the party genuinely had shifted to the left ever so slightly from its even less savoury policies. Only a spell in power could put the opposing opinions to task.

At the time the country was, as it had been since it regained political stability after the war, under a coalition government. The coalition was formed between the two main parties, the Social Democrats and the conservative People's Party. Nationally, the Freedom Party was not in a position to influence politics to much of a degree, although, as Haider himself exemplified, they attained certain local and regional power. Like all populists, however, Haider was on the same wavelength as a good deal of the electorate when he started criticising the country's immigration policies. The party's showings in opinion polls started to raise eyebrows not only in Austrian liberal society but also in the outside world. As the October 1999 election approached, polls predicted Haider's party winning between 25% and 30% of the vote.

To the rest of the world, there was a real threat that a European Union country would have a Nazi at its helm, even though few respected commentators would seriously brand Haider a Nazi in any historical sense. Nevertheless, European and American politicians urged Austrians to resist Haider's populist rhetoric and to vote for any party but his.

Whether influenced positively or negatively by such external pressure, Austrians voted on 3 October and Haider's Freedom Party came second with 27.2% of the vote, entitling it to 52 of the 183 seats. The Social Democrats technically won with 33.3%, and the conservative People's Party came third with 26.9%, but the result meant that no party had overall control. The Social Democrats, under the existing Chancellor, Victor Klima, tried and failed to form a coalition with the third-place People's Party, and to hold power as a minority government, all of which left the country without effective government.

For Jorg Haider, however, power was within his grasp if he himself could form a coalition of his own, and the natural ally would be the conservatives. Negotiations started between the two parties who in combination could claim to represent 54% of the electorate.

Anti-Austrian activity intensified. Then US president Bill Clinton and the British prime minister Tony Blair urged the People's Party not to enter into any power-sharing deals with the Freedom Party. In the UK the Anti-Nazi League urged businesses to pull out of Austria if such a coalition was formed, at least until Haider's party lost power. In Austria, the former president, Kurt Waldheim, effectively told the rest of the world to mind its own business and to at least give the coalition a chance. It was a sentiment that received wide agreement in Austria.

On 31 January 2001, The European Commission issued a statement saying that it would isolate Austria if Haider was allowed to form a government. There was even talk of outright expulsion or suspension. The next day, however, the EC markedly softened its stance, saying that punishment would only be inflicted if Austria broke the European Union laws on human rights, which put forward the message that a coalition with Haider was perfectly acceptable, albeit with an automatic "two strikes" to his name, in baseball parlance. The situation certainly raised serious questions about individual member states' right to vote for whomever they chose. Haider angrily retorted that should such measures be taken, he would bring the EU to a standstill by exercising Austria's veto whenever possible.

Four months after the elections, on 4 February, 2000, the Freedom Party and the People's Party at last agreed to form a coalition, with the Freedom Party holding most of the major departments, including Defence, Justice, Finance and Social Affairs. Haider himself chose not to be part of the cabinet, preferring instead to retain his governorship of Carinthia, possibly to placate international objectors, although his personal presidential, rather than prime ministerial, aspirations might have played their part. He remained head of the party. Wolfgang Schussel, leader of the People's Party, became Chancellor. The US and Israel promptly recalled their ambassadors from Vienna.

On 28 February 2000, Jorg Haider, under immense international and Europe-wide pressure, quit as leader of the party, but continued in post as governor of Carinthia.

So the raw statement that Austria elected a fascist as its leader does not necessarily hold true. Although 27 per cent of the vote is by no means insignificant, representing the views of over one in four voters, the political situation, one of perpetual coalition and radical stagnation, certainly fertilised the shoots of right-wing opinion. It was in effect a three-way split between liberals, conservatives and the far right, which certainly puts the mean position somewhere right of centre, which might suggest that illiberal or even racist views might enjoy greater tolerance. The fact that Austrian liberals did not seem capable of mobilising a knockout blow to the far right in the face of international condemnation and warning is noteworthy. In the French presidential elections of 2002, the far right candidate Jean-Marie Le Pen eliminated the liberal incumbent, Lionel Jospin, in the penultimate round of voting, making the final round a head-to-head fight between Le Pen and the right of centre Jacques Chirac. Jospin urged his supporters to swallow their pride and vote for Chirac; this, marches and an enormous popular effort made sure that Le Pen and his policies were trounced in the final round. Nothing like this had happened in Austria. Of course, apathy and complacency can share their parts of the blame, and perhaps the very example of Jorg Haider two years earlier ignited the French, but the fact remains that a quarter of those who voted chose a populist, anti-immigration, hard-line nationalist to be leader of their country, and the reasons behind these millions of individual decisions certainly need to be looked into.

The situation also served to highlight a flaw in the principle of democracy, a political philosophy that is pushed relentlessly at the world. The ancient Greeks had a form of democracy that allowed only men of a certain class to vote; suffrage was not much wider in the Roman Empire. A democracy as we know it today is a state where all citizens above a certain age and fulfilling various other criteria (for example not being in prison) are allowed to elect its leaders. I can see four simple problems with this system. First, manifestoes are not legally-binding documents, which means that a party's election campaigns can be fought on whatever populist issue or opposition-hammering measure takes its fancy, but there will be no punishment if promises are not kept. Second, not all voters are intelligent, rational beings and many will vote for personalities over policies or single issues over a broad spectrum. Third, after several decades of democracy in a country, the electable parties are usually reduced to two very strong, seemingly polarised parties, with all other parties becoming unelectable due to a fear of a "wasted vote". These dominant parties ultimately start to converge politically to fight over a perceived "middle ground", chasing voters over specific fringe issues, but leaving vast swaths of the electorate (usually the poor and powerless) effectively disenfranchised; those that do vote tend to go for the party they perceive as closest to them rather than the one that reflects their views, in a measure to avoid the least-liked of the choices. Independent candidates have an uphill battle if they are to out-voice the main parties' messages; they need funding, media attention and support conjured from effectively nowhere. Fourth, the party system that inevitably takes over politics reduces people's choice to two supposedly unified bodies of candidates with a huge array of policies. This way a party with several popular key policies might be elected despite the almost hidden presence of dozens of less well known but altogether unsavoury policies.

For a free democracy to thrive, therefore, there needs to be free, independent, press and broadcast media, good quality, modern education free from political and religious influences, and accountability and transparency. Voters need to think that their vote really does count, and most constituency-based systems alienate people whose views are not strongly supported in the area in which they live. Proportional representation, on the other hand, makes it difficult to allocate parliamentary seats, but it is possible to work out a fair system. However, all this comes to nothing when popular national newspapers and television news broadcasters are supported by, favour or have affiliations with a particular party. They can print party propaganda and present it as facts and as news, knowing that large percentages of their readerships will believe the story regardless, even after it has been proved to be at worst plain wrong or at best editorial opinion. Unless the electorate has access to independent, verifiable sources of news, democracy does not have a hope, and is effectively in the hands of a small number of media barons. Every dictator knows that ownership of the media is an unquestionable requirement; in most states that proudly boast of their press freedom, however, large media organisations can effectively block out anti-government voices while at the same time apparently maintain distance from the government. It is difficult to see how true freedom and democracy can exist in such circumstances. Perhaps the example of Austria in 1999 and 2000 should be a warning that democracy needs to be constantly worked on for it to be successful, otherwise it is democracy in name only.

For my part, which is really all I have to go on, I was treated dreadfully by the Austrians. What I have to come to terms with is the question whether it was me personally that inspired such hatred, the fact that I am an Arab, the fact that I escaped and opposed Saddam, or a combination of all three. Would I have received the same treatment if I was a European who had escaped Ceausescu's Romania, for example? There is no way of knowing. It is worth bearing in mind that the Austrians did indeed have strong political links with the regime that engulfed me, which could at a stretch suggest a lack of racial hatred. But when the country in question also happens to be an oil producing one, led by a man who was a Muslim and an Arab when it suited him, and not when it hindered him, who actively oppressed Arabs, Kurds and Muslims in general, it should water down any such suggestive conclusions about Austria's welcoming stance towards Baghdad.

For every racist, torturing Austrian I met, there were ten open-minded, peaceful ones. What seems to be lacking is a strong, persuasive opposition to the attitudes that saw me imprisoned and humiliated. Perhaps this failure to react to racist, nationalistic attitudes is a passive or active acceptance of such opinions. Perhaps the immigration argument really does need to be looked at seriously, as it does in every country, only without xenophobic, populist and racist undertones. But for the time being at least, I would suggest that Austria has some work to do if it wants the rest of the world to see it as a progressive member of the international community. If my contribution to the argument opens anyone's eyes to the sickness at the heart of the country, then my decision to publish this story might prove worthwhile.

*   *   *   *   *

In Chapter 5 I gave an account of my meeting with the Kuwaiti representatives charged with locating the 650 prisoners taken by Iraq during the first Gulf War. They had been told by "reliable sources" that they were alive and well, and by me that they had been murdered. (Among the sources was al-Chalabi, who reliably informed the US that Saddam had weapons of mass destruction in the run-up to the 2003 Gulf War.) When Saddam fell at the end of the war, and Iraq was under US occupation, the Kuwaitis got their first chance to find out which of their informants was telling the truth. Unfortunately for the families, it was me. Kuwaiti agents used my maps to locate mass graves and identified the victims, who had been dead for years, held hostage only in the minds of the families, their ransoms paid to the people who planted their phantoms there.

How many millions of people had been lied to? How many had longed for the day when their bedraggled, emaciated but breathing loved ones, colleagues and compatriots would be brought back home to heroes' welcomes?

After the discoveries I was contacted by Kuwaiti officials. They thanked me for telling them the truth. After all the hope they had been given, my news had not been welcome. There could even have been an element of denial in it, or perhaps the weight of evidence I could provide had been balanced or outdone by that of the opposition.

"After all the letters from prisoners," they told me, "the assurances, it was hard to take. It hurt."

"Did you pay the people who fed you the information?" I asked, even though I was sure of the answer.

"Yes. People will pay anything for information. Especially when it is good news."

"There you are," I said with a grimace. "Did I ask for any money for my information? No. I told you the truth because I am a human and because one day the truth was always destined to come out. I did it for the people filled with hope, as the more hopes are allowed to build up, the greater the despair when they are dashed."

Months later, I was sitting in my home when the doorbell rang. I answered it, and there was the secretary to the ambassador of the Prince of Kuwait.

"Latif," he began, "I have a present from the Prince."

"What kind of present?" I asked. I had no idea what he was talking about.

He took me out and we eventually turned into a street where was parked a beautiful red Rolls-Royce 95, a two-door cabriolet, the value of which I knew to be about £100,000.

"Here is the key," he announced, holding out his hand to me and smiling.

I was astounded. "First of all," I gulped, "thank you very much." I gazed at the lines of the car and shuddered at the opulence painted within them. I continued: "But I can't accept it." I wanted to be careful not to appear ungrateful, but under the circumstances I could not take the gift. What would it have been for? Telling the truth? Witnessing the murders in the first place had been a chance occurrence, not the result of my hard work or any benevolent motives. I had been forced into it, and I had merely used my knowledge to tell the Kuwaitis the truth. Until the meeting at the Kuwaiti ambassador's I would have assumed that the Kuwaitis already knew the truth.

Seven days later, the Prince of Kuwait himself arrived in London for an appointment with a medical practitioner. While in the country he asked the ambassador if he could locate me. I was called by the ambassador.

"The Prince of Kuwait is in the country," he reported, "and he has asked by name to see you. You have eleven minutes to meet him." My eleven minutes were not as imminent as they sounded. The meeting was to take place when he returned home. Apparently an audience with the Prince had been requested by various members of the Iraqi opposition who were roughing it in London. The Prince had refused them all.

I met the Prince in one of his enormous palaces – those sprawling, pillared, air-conditioned homages to the ancient rulers that dot London. He was a very old man at the time, incapable of walking. When he saw me enter the room, he beckoned me over weakly.

"Mr. Yahia," he said. "Thank you very much for the information. In Kuwait we have opened a new page with you. You, and anyone you bring with you, will be my guest in my country any time you might wish to come to Kuwait.

This holds for today and in the future, and over every ministry in the whole of Kuwait."

"Thank you very much," I replied.

"But tell me, Mr. Yahia, why did you not accept my present?"

"It was nothing personal, nothing to do with you or your country. I was very humbled and grateful, but I simply could not accept it. I cannot accept any kind of reward for information such as I gave, and I have decided that I never will."

He nodded appreciatively. "Here is a letter," he said, sliding the folded paper towards me. "It is a letter signed by me and will ensure that you will always be a guest in Kuwait. And this applies after I have gone."

I received a similar "honour" from the Saudi royal family, many of whose subjects' graves I also helped to locate. They have very short memories, or treat life with such contempt that they must imagine that everyone else does too. It will not come as a surprise to learn that the Saudis' gratitude was limited and conditional – they would not even allow my first book, I was Saddam's son, on the shelves of their bookstores. Even in Kuwait one could buy my book (although the profits from that country's sales were donated to a Kuwaiti orphanage). The book would have been allowed in Saudi Arabia if I were to agree to some censorship. Some of the "offensive" parts pointed out the similarities and differences between Saddam Hussein and King Fahad, and tarnished the pure, shiny image that was put to the Saudi nationals from on high. Mystifyingly, other parts about Bedouins were in addition deemed unsuitable. My book would have amounted to an advertisement for King Fahad. I could not accept this deal, and to this day the book is forbidden there.

My chances of having this book published there are, to be optimistic, non-existent as long as the current regime remains in power. When work opposing the regime is written, their banning it simply lends credibility to the arguments presented therein, whereas allowing it to be published would give them a chance to rebut, even rubbish, them. No doubt they will instead continue to make their choice based on the most simple-minded reasoning.

* * * * *

As for my cousin – who had been an ardent follower of Jalal Talabani in his struggle for freedom in northern Iraq, and who, in his well-meaning but blundering way, helped me so thanklessly in my first days in Austria – he is now a full-time doctor. His association with Talabani ended when I sat him down one day and told him some truths about the person for whom he was acting as a spokesman. He did not have any inkling that he might be corrupt and that he had been on Saddam's payroll, or that he was just as culpable as the other tribal leaders for the flare-ups that brought death and mayhem to the region he purportedly aimed to pacify. My cousin needed some convincing, but the photograph of Talabani with "Uday", soon after receiving the 25 million dinar donation, certainly helped.

I wish them both the very best of luck in their chosen paths.

- A Special Thanks -

I would like to take this opportunity to thank everyone in the International media who made it possible for me to bring my story to the world in1992 and later give me the chance to voice my opposition to the war on Iraq in 2003.

3SAT TV (GER)
ABC News (USA)
Al –Wasat Magazine(Lonodn UK)
Al-Ahram International Newspaper (Egypt)
Al-Hadath Newspaper (Jordan)
Al-Hayat Newspaper(London UK)
Al-Jazeera TV (London UK) Arabic channel
Al-Kabis Newspaper (Kuwait)
Al-Majaless magazine (Kuwait)
Al-Quds Al-Arabi Newspaper (London UK)
Al-Watan International Newspaper (Kuwait)
ARTE (GER)
Ashaq Al-Awsat Newspaper (London UK)
Associated Press News Agen
BBC World (UK)
BBC TV (UK)
BBC Radio (UK)
BILD Newspaper(GER)
Boulevarde Bio. ARD (GER)
Breakfast with Frost. BBC (UK)
BVN TV (NL)
CBC TV (Canada)
CBS TV(USA)
CNN TV(US)
Daily Mail Newspaper (UK)

Das Magazin (Switz)
Dubai TV (UAE)
DW TV (GER)
El Pais Newspaper (Spain)
ESPN (USA)
Figaro Newspaper (FRA)
Fox News (US)
France Presse News agency
HA'ARETZ Newspaper (ISRAEL)
Heimat Und Welt Newspaper (Austria)
Ireland AM. TV3 (IRE)
Irish Examiner. Newspaper (IRE)
Irish Sunday Mirror Newspaper (IRE)
Kurier Newspaper (Austria)
La Nacional Newspaper (CHILE)
LBC TV (Lebanon)
Le Monde Newspaaper (FRA)
Ma'arif Newspaper (ISRAEL)
Mail on Sunday Newspaper (UK)
MBC (Lonodn UK) Arabic Channel
Munchen Runde. BR TV (GER)
N24 News (GER)
NBC News (USA)
Network TV (NL)
NEWS magazine (AUSTRIA)
Newsweek magazine (US)
NINE NETWORK TV (Australia)
Nordlandsposten Newspaper (NOR)
Nova TV (Belgium)
Observer Newspaper (Austria)
Panorama with John Simpson BBC (UK)
Playboy magazine (GER)
Primera TV (GER)
Pro 7 TV (GER)
PROFIL Newspaper (GER)
Reuters News agency

Richard and Judy. Channel 4 TV (UK)
RTE Gerry Ryan Show Radio (IRE)
RTL TV(GER)
RTL 2 TV (GER)
Sabah El Kheir magazine (Egypt)
SAT 1 TV (GER)
NHK TV (Japan)
SKY News (UK)
STERN TV (GER)
Tempo magazine (GER)
The Financial Times Newspaper (UK)
The Gerry Kelly show. UTV (N.IRE)
The Gerry Ryan show. RTE Radio (IRE)
The Guardian Newspaper (UK)
The Independent Newspaper (UK)
The Irish Independent Newspaper (IRE)
The Irish Times Newspaper (IRE)
The STAR Newspaper (IRE)
The Irish Mirror Newspaper IRE)
The Los Angeles Times Newspaper (USA)
The New York Times Newspaper (USA)
The Sunday Independent Newspaper (IRE)
The Sunday Telegraph (UK)
The Sunday Times Newspaper (UK)
The WALL STREET JOURNAL Newspaper (US)
The Washington Post Newspaper (USA)
TIME magazine (USA)
The Express Newspaper (UK)
The Scotsman Newspaper (SCOT)
Tonight with Trevor Mc Donald. ITV (UK)
Tros TV (NL)
TV Belgium (Belgium)
TV2 (DEN)
TV2 (NOR)
TV 5 (FRA)
Der Spiegel Newspaper (GER)

USA Today Newspaper (US)
VG Newspaper (NOR)
YEDIOTH AHRONOT Newspaper (ISRAEL)
ZDF TV (GER)

Again many thanks to all of the above and if I have omitted anyone my apologies.

Latif Yahia

The Black Hole